Anita began her journey in her native Romania, survived the Nazis and the Communist takeover of her country. As emigrants, armed only with a piece of paper typed in Romanian, as they had to relinquish Romanian citizenship, she left Romania at the age of 10, with her mother and grandmother for Israel, Cuba, and Canada. Years later, as a doctoral student at Cornell University, she fell in love with a Fulbright scholar from South Africa, Denis Worrall, and followed him to South Africa, a land in the midst of apartheid.

She shared her politician and diplomat husband's passion for transforming the land of apartheid to full democracy. The story embodies the essence of resilience in the midst of challenging times, from the reality of being Jewish in the first half of the twentieth century and the journey to end apartheid in the land Anita made her home.

Dr Anita Worrall is an internationally acclaimed educational psychologist and a specialist in children with learning difficulties. She is the founder of Pro Ed Centre and Pro Ed House School in Cape Town. During the last 40 years, she and her colleagues have helped boys and girls overcome their learning difficulties and thus to realize their potential.

To Denis, whose life I was fortunate to share.

To our sons, Chris, Lyndon, and Dean and to our grandchildren. May they show the resilience of their great-grandmother, Rose, whose sacrifices and determination made it all possible.

Anita Worrall

A RESILIENT MINDSET

Anita's Story

AUSTIN MACAULEY PUBLISHERS™

LONDON ★ CAMBRIDGE ★ NEW YORK ★ SHARJAH

Ordering Information
Quantity sales: Special discounts are available on quantity purchases by corporations, associations, and others. For details, contact the publisher at the address below.

Publisher's Cataloging-in-Publication data
Worrall, Anita
A Resilient Mindset

ISBN 9798889103752 (Paperback)
ISBN 9798889103769 (ePub e-book)

Library of Congress Control Number: 2023920479

www.austinmacauley.com/us

First Published 2024
Austin Macauley Publishers LLC
40 Wall Street, 33rd Floor, Suite 3302
New York, NY 10005
USA

mail-usa@austinmacauley.com
+1 (646) 5125767

My husband, Denis, an accomplished writer, lovingly scrutinized every page of this manuscript. Throughout our married life, he has consistently been my best critic and confidence booster.

This book could not have been written without the dedication and skill of Deborah Bennett throughout the long journey.

To Russell Martin many thanks for your counsel before and during the writing of this memoir.

I would like to thank Valery Ribakow, the cover artist, and Anthony Cuerden, who selected it.

Table of Contents

Foreword By Tony Leon — 14

Preface By Colette Avital — 17

Author's Note — 19

Chapter 1: My Birth and Early Years — 20

My Mother's Family — 21

My Aunt Gisela — 22

My Father's Family — 24

My Parents Marry — 25

Romania at the Time of My Birth — 26

The Tragedy of the Struma — 29

Chapter 2: Romania Is Liberated — 31

Life Under the New Regime — 33

Chapter 3: Leaving Romania — 37

The Trip — 38

The Journey to Israel — 39

Chapter 4: Life in Israel in 1950 — 41

Life for Me in Tel Aviv Was Exciting — 43

School in Jaffa — 44

Chapter 5: We Fly to Havana   **60**

Sojourn in Havana   *61*

Stranded in Havana   *63*

I Make a Big Discovery   *63*

School in Havana   *65*

Chapter 6: On the Way to Montréal   **66**

Chapter 7: Montréal   **68**

Montréal High School for Girls   *69*

Living in Montréal   *71*

Our New Life   *73*

McGill University   *74*

Chapter 8: Cornell University   **78**

Social Life at Cornell   *80*

Chapter 9: Romance with Denis   **83**

We Say Goodbye   *87*

An Airletter Romance   *87*

I Use the Reparation Money   *88*

Chapter 10: I Arrive in South Africa   **90**

Chapter 11: Meeting Denis' Family   **94**

Our Wedding Day   *95*

Chapter 12: Durban: Our Home for a While   **97**

Chapter 13: Life in Pretoria   **100**

Working on My Dissertation   *103*

Chapter 14: New Nation	**107**

Chapter 15: I Embark on a New Career	**111**

**Chapter 16: We Move to Johannesburg
and Become Parents**	**126**

*We Move to Grahamstown and Our
Little Family Grows*	*129*

**Chapter 17: We Move to Cape Town but Contest
an Election in Durban**	**133**

Gardens Constituency	*135*

Chapter 18: I Go Back to Work	**139**

*The President's Council and Our Departure
for Australia*	*141*

The Move to the President's Council	*143*

Chapter 19: Preparations to Leave for Australia	**146**

Chapter 20: We Arrive in Australia	**149**

We Settle Down in Canberra	*152*

We Leave for London	*155*

Chapter 21: We Arrive in London	**159**

Our Official Residence in London—Highveld	*162*

We Settle in London	*168*

**Chapter 22: Getting Acquainted with the United
Kingdom: A Startling Beginning**	**191**

Travels to Scotland and Northern Ireland	*192*

Celebrating Shakespeare's Birthday	*194*

Social Life in London   196

*Family Holidays and Denis
Increasingly Frustrated*   200

Chapter 23: The Eminent Persons Group (EPG)   203

Denis Resigns   205

**Chapter 24: Federation of International Women's
Associations of London (FIWAL)**   210

I Travel to China and to Harare   212

Chapter 25: I Go Back to Romania   217

**Chapter 26: I Return to Pro Ed Center and
Start a New School**   222

We Open Pro Ed House School   225

**Chapter 27: A Thinking School: Transforming
Education in South Africa**   230

References   235

What are the factors that help some adults to bounce back while others languish in feelings of helplessness and hopelessness? Why do some individuals attain success that could never have been predicted from their life circumstances? What is the inner strength that propels some people to overcome mighty obstacles in their path?

The Power of Resilience—Robert Brooks, Ph.D. and Sam Goldstein, Ph.D.

It's the circle of life
It's the wheel of fortune
It's the leap of faith
It's the band of hope
Till we find our place
On the path unwinding, yeah
In the circle, the circle of life.

A song from Disney's, The Lion King, 1994, Elton John and Tim Rice.

Foreword
By Tony Leon

Novelist Julian Barnes wrote, *Most of us have only one story to tell. I don't mean that only one thing happened to us in our lives: there are countless events, which we turn into countless stories. But there is only one that matters, only one that is finally worth telling.*

Anita Worrall's memoirs which you are about to read combine the singularity of her remarkable life and its improbable arc and the many locations in which it is set; her tangled origins, and her quite extraordinary resilience and adaptiveness. These have the makings of several plotlines for a good novel.

Instead, Anita's real-life story which she tells with both verve and a welcome absence of sentimentality is an object lesson in survival and then triumph in the most improbable of circumstances.

Her childhood was in Nazi-aligned Romania during the Second World War—not a promising start to life for a child of Jewish parentage (the subject of her real father is quite simply a story on its own which she tells here), born into the vanishing bourgeois world. Then to the rigors of newly-born Israel, and to give real meaning to the adage of 'the wandering Jew (ess)', Anita then describes life in Cuba before the revolution and Canada before its full immersion into multiculturalism. And all this in her first two decades of life.

In fact, and as this book attests, Anita has lived and experienced no fewer than eight countries and studies and speaks no fewer than six languages.

Because of Anita's long and enduring marriage to the former South African politician and diplomat Denis Worrall, South Africa became and remains her home and her arrival here in the mid-1960s is both well described and vividly recalled. No less so the possibilities and pitfalls of being married to an eminent political figure and ambassador in whose career she was certainly a co-partner.

The real worth of this book is that it reminds readers that Anita was not simply the tag-along 'plus one' in her husband's career, but a pioneering counseling and educational psychologist and a mother of three sons, each of whom she nurtured with both intellectual and emotional sustenance.

In a world where victimology is all too frequent an excuse for lack of achievement or progress, Anita's story is a worthy rebuttal of how to overcome difficult circumstance and to achieve success.

On a personal note, I was her husband Denis' successor as leader of the Democratic Party, but far more relevant to this book, my wife Michal is the daughter of parents, who like Anita were born in Romania and survived the Nazi regime there and then, just as she did, emigrated to Israel to escape the heel of communism. Synchronicity indeed!

(Tony Leon served as leader of the official opposition in the parliament of South Africa and was founding leader of the Democratic Alliance. Thereafter, he was appointed as Ambassador to Argentina, Uruguay, and Paraguay. He is the author of five books, of which the most recent is *Future Tense—Reflections on my Troubled Land*, Jonathan Ball Publishers.)

Preface
By Colette Avital

This is the unusual story of the road to success of a little girl, Anita, who was my friend, and who, against all odds survived under the worst circumstances of the twentieth century: Nazi persecution, communist repression, the pangs and tribulations of immigration, poverty, closed borders. Born to a Jewish family in Romania, she witnesses the cruelty of both Nazi and Romanian fascist perpetrators, then the Stalinist totalitarian rule; so, like for many, the State of Israel becomes the only way to freedom. But Israel in the 50s is a new country, beset by economic and security problems and has no means to absorb properly the million refugees that have doubled its population.

Anita's mother is the extraordinary figure who with much courage and determination manages to lead the family to Canada and to give her a proper life and education. This is also the extraordinary story of a young woman who chooses to follow the love of her life, alone, to an unknown country, who joins and supports his relentless struggle to make South Africa a better, more just society. But this in itself would not satisfy the strong and ambitious woman that Anita has become: she pursues her own career as an educational psychologist, bringing innovation to her field, and contributing to the well-being of children in her new adoptive country. Told with utmost candor, this is a saga of ultimate optimism, a fascinating book that will enrich all those who will have the privilege to read it.

(Ambassador Colette Avital, Romanian-Israeli diplomat, and politician.)

Author's Note

This is my story and the story of my family. Many people have asked me to write it down. My story is set in the middle of the twentieth century in Eastern Europe, at the time of the persecution of the Jewish people, followed by the communist regimes. Together with my family, we escaped from Romania by way of Israel and Cuba to land in Montréal, Canada. I graduated from McGill University and studied at Cornell University where I met my future South African husband, Denis Worrall, a Fulbright student.

He promised me that South Africa would change and in no small way, he contributed to that change.

My training had been in psychology and I pursued my career running a multidisciplinary clinic and a school for children with learning disabilities. Together with my colleagues, teachers, and therapists, I have the satisfaction of knowing that many boys and girls have benefited from our teachings and have been able to meet their wonderful potential.

It is a story that is attached to the millennia long story of the Jewish people. It is a story of resilience, of taking risks and of courage to move to uncertain futures and strange lands.

Chapter 1
My Birth and Early Years

I was born into a Jewish family in Bucharest, Romania in 1938. My mother used to say that I was born the day Hitler marched into Vienna following the Anschluss—a slight mistake with the dates. Hitler marched into Vienna on 12 March, and I was born on the 13th. Bucharest at that time was a beautiful city. In fact, it was highly sophisticated and cultured and known as 'The Paris of the East'. But it is a sign of that time that my mother would think of Hitler and Vienna in relation to my birth date. Although antisemitism was always an undercurrent in Romania, this was shortly to change and change dramatically as first the fascists and then the communists took over. These were very turbulent times. My family, secular, cosmopolitan with deep roots in Romania, managed to survive, but not before virulent pogroms, bombings, humiliations, and loss of assets. They loved me and protected me all their lives and therefore the small tribute.

My Mother's Family

My mother, Rose Kimelman, known in the family as Rosie, was a beautiful woman. She was the second of four children of Marie and Bernard Kimelman and was born in Czernowitz, then part of the Habsburg Crownland of Bukovina, where my grandparents met and fell in love. Czernowitz, part of present-day Ukraine, had a reputation of being a 'little Vienna'. Fashionable ladies went to Czernowitz to purchase their outfits from famous designers. My grandmother, Omama to me, and her sisters, would go there for seasonal purchases.

Once married, my grandparents set up house in Czernowitz and had two daughters, Gisela, and my mother Rose. They were followed by a daughter Dida and a son Joseph but called Nelu. Probably, because of the approaching war, the family moved to Bucharest, where they had a beautiful big house next to Notre Dame de Zion, a girls' school run by nuns. My mother attended the school, and later, I attended it too. My family was not particularly religious and the Kimelman girls were very happy at Notre Dame de Zion School. The nuns knew my mother well and called her Rosica, a diminutive of Rosie. The nuns were forced to leave Romania when the communists took over.

My grandmother, Omama Marie, was born in Romania, in the town of Bacau, where my great-grandfather Menachem Gross owned a large textile factory. During WWI, the Romanian government purchased material for army uniforms from my great-grandfather's factory. My grandfather, Bernard, came from Galicia, on the west part of what is presently Ukraine, probably from Lemberg (present day Lviv). We never met his family and, as far as we know, they were all murdered during the Holocaust.

My grandfather was an Austrian citizen and German-speaking and the Kimelman family spoke mostly German at home. At the beginning of WWI, because he was considered to be an 'enemy alien', he was arrested in Bucharest and placed in a refugee camp. He returned after 1917 but was very ill and died not long afterwards. My mother often described to me the scene when she was five years old and was playing in the garden. She saw what was to her a stranger approaching. Frightened, she wanted to run inside, but the man said, "Rosica, ich bin dein Vader." This memory remained with her for the rest of her life. After my grandfather died, Omama had to fend for the family. Yet her children attended private schools and she was even able to engage several university students as tutors. These Jewish students were mostly poor and attracted to communism. Some fought for the Republicans in Spain and some for the communists in Russia. They were handsomely rewarded after the war when they returned to Romania. My mother was to meet them in very different circumstances.

My Aunt Gisela

My mother's older sister Gisela was an opera singer. My grandparents sent her to Italy to study further. She sang at the Scala Opera House in Milan. Unfortunately, Italy under Mussolini, discriminated against Jews and Gisela sought refuge in a convent. She was eternally grateful to the nuns and converted to Catholicism.

I am unsure how they met, but soon after WWII ended, Gisela married an American journalist of Albanian descent, Michael Chinigo, who later became the European Director of International News Services. Gisela and he lived in Rome and Chinigo, it seems, persuaded Mrs. Mussolini to write her memoirs.

Many years later, I read that, although of Albanian descent and an American citizen, Chinigo was born in Calabria, Italy. He is described 'rather colorfully' in Maureen Hughes book, *The Countess and the Mob,* as a spy, diplomat, and journalist, who worked for the OSS and the CIA.[1] The story is fascinating. Apparently, he had met my aunt Gisela shortly after the liberation of Sicily, which he covered for the newspapers. They were married shortly afterwards and in 1946, Gisela invited Omama to visit her in Rome. Omama spent six months with the Chinigos. She met Mrs. Mussolini at Gisela's house and was full of wonderful tales of their life in Rome when she returned to Bucharest. Their apartment on Via Monte Parioli was visited by the best and brightest of Roman society. Gisela was a frequent visitor to the Vatican and was one of their most devoted society ladies.

Sadly, my aunt died of cancer in 1952, while we were in Havana. I remember the date, as this was when Evita Peron also succumbed to cancer. Havana was in deep mourning. Shortly after we arrived in Montréal, Michael Chinigo sent us two trunk loads of beautiful things that had belonged to my aunt. I read that he later became involved with the Mafia! As a widower, he married an American socialite but divorced soon afterwards. He was reported to have been gunned down by the Mafia and buried next to Gisela in Rome.

My Father's Family

My father, George Iancu, was the youngest son of Herman and Rachel Iancu. They also had a daughter, Lucia (Medi), and two more sons. The eldest son, Marcel, was one of the founding members of the Dada Movement in Zürich in 1916. The three brothers were students during most of WWI. There were many Romanian students in Zürich at that time. Tom Sandqvist wrote a book called *Dada East— The Romanians of Cabaret Voltaire,* a nightclub where they used to meet and perform.[2] My husband, Denis, and I searched for Cabaret Voltaire during a visit we made to Zürich. We found it almost opposite the house in which the Russian leader, Lenin lived when in exile in Zürich. The Iancu brothers, along with many other Romanian students, lived cheek to jowl with Lenin and a future foreign minister of Romania, Ana Pauker.

To my astonishment, when visiting Cabaret Voltaire, we discovered a large noticeboard upstairs on which there was an old black and white photograph of a well-dressed, handsome man, whom I recognized to be my uncle Marcel. When I asked the staff who the man was, they said they had no idea. They were intrigued when I told them that he was my uncle, Marcel Janco, one of the founders of the famous Dada Art Movement.

They asked us to return the next morning and we were shown some books and photographs relating to Marcel Janco and Dadaism and they insisted that we take several of the books with us. Marcel and his second brother, Jules, changed their name Iancu to the more Western European version, Janco. Although not recognized in Romania, most Romanians living in Europe have changed their names ending in 'u' to 'o', for example, Ionesco, Enesco, and so forth.

My grandfather, Herman, was a prominent merchant, one of the few occupations allowed to Jews in Romania at the time. The family was well off and could afford to send their three sons to study in Switzerland. They were assimilated Jews, living outside of the 'Jewish quarter' and by the time I was born, they were living, as the writer Sandqvist describes it, *in one of Bucharest's large private houses with a garden of several thousand square meters.* Incidentally, that garden is one of my earliest memories. I must have heard the adults expressing anxiety about certain events because my memory of the garden is associated with a feeling of angst. I have a photograph of myself in that garden. I must have been about two years old.

My Parents Marry

My mother was 23 years old when she met Engineer George Iancu. She was part of a group of close friends, most of whom were about to marry and emigrate shortly afterwards. Although she was in love with a young man, Aristide (Tidy) Calmi, who had returned from Paris, where he had studied politics and economics at the University of Sorbonne, my mother was pressed into getting married to George Iancu, as her mother was running out of money. Years later, she told me how on the eve of the wedding,

Tidy had visited her and had begged her not to marry George. Young and naive, she said she couldn't disappoint her mother and the Iancu family. And so, she married George in 1936. She moved into the Iancu home with Grandmother Rachel, something which later had considerable complications.

Romania at the Time of My Birth

It was a difficult time for the Jewish population of Bucharest in 1938. Mihail Sebastian`s Journal from 1935 to1944 describes the years immediately prior to my birth and a few years afterwards.[3] Sebastian was Jewish, but an assimilated intellectual. He kept a diary of the events, during which three antisemitic dictatorships succeeded each other with devastating results for the Jewish population of Romania. For example, his entry in February 1938, shortly before my birth, describes the atmosphere in Bucharest as 'feverish'. There were doubts, rumors, and anxious nights. News from Germany and Austria was frightening and absurd.

His entry on Thursday, 17 March 1938, mentions that Freud, described as a 'pseudo scientist', had been arrested in Vienna by the Nazis. Sebastian and his fellow Jews were 'anxious, dazzled and disorientated'.

During World War II, approximately 300,000 Jewish people were murdered in Romania. The deportations, shootings and starvations occurred mostly in what were territories granted to Romania after WWI. The Romanian dictator, Ion Antonescu, was in favor of racial purification of Romania, but by 1941, although Romania was a member of the Axis, he feared that Germany would lose the war. Furthermore, he was anxious not to disrupt the economy as it was very reliant on Jewish skills. Although the Jewish population of Bucharest was not deported, it was subjected to forced labor, heavy taxes, and confiscation of property. My first cousin Raimond (Bodu), the son of my father's sister, was called to do forced labor while still a student. One of the supervisors decided that Bodu was not working hard enough, and he pushed him in the path of an oncoming train. Fortunately, my cousin was fast enough to avoid the train, but not before part of his foot was cut off.

The Iron Guard was a major political and intellectual force in Romania between 1930 and 1941. It was anti-democratic, anti-capitalist, anti-communist and antisemitic. Guardians served in Antonescu's cabinet. In January 1941, the Iron Guard revolted against Antonescu's regime and declared death to all Jewish intellectuals. This resulted in a pogrom, termed 'Kristaalnacht of Bucharest'. Sebastian in his diary described it as 'the shooting never-ending'.

My mother carrying me, a two-year old child decided it was not safe to stay in the Iancu family home, as the family was known in Bucharest to be prominent members of the Jewish community. She took a taxi to go to Omama. Fortunately, the taxi driver was more interested in the fare than in her being Jewish. All her life, my mother recalled that terrible night and how fortunate she had been, as many others who took a taxi in similar circumstances were taken directly to their slaughter. And slaughter it was. My father's brother, Marcel Iancu, who was still in Bucharest at that time, described looking for his brother-in-law's friend, a well-known journalist. He found him strung up at the slaughterhouse, where other prominent Jewish intellectuals ended up that night.

I don't remember the details, but in June 1941, as Germany invaded Russia and Romania concluded a pact with Germany, we experienced the first Russian bombardment. I recall being in my grandmother Marie's apartment which had a bomb shelter underneath. As my mother and I went hurtling down the stairs to the shelter, I recall telling my mother with chattering teeth and in a babyish voice, *"Nu fi flica, mama, nu fi flica mama,"* ("don't be afraid, mama, don't be afraid, mama.") In Romanian, the word should be 'frica', but I could not yet pronounce the letter 'r'. This is my earliest memory. A memory built on fear!

As a baby, I was blonde. My grandmother Rachel had a driver by the name of Lungianu. He was married to a German girl, who was my nanny. One day, when I was about ten months old, as she strolled with me in the park, she was stopped by some German soldiers who asked her permission to take a photo of me to send back to Germany as 'a real German baby in Romania!' Very amused, she returned home to tell my mother.

The driver Lungianu was an opportunist of the worst kind. Just about every night, he would wake Grandmother Rachel to tell her that he'd heard from his friends at the police station, that that night they were going to arrest my father. In order to stop them, he was required to pay them money. And so it went, and my grandmother paid so many bribes that by the end of the war, she hardly had any money left.

My uncles Marcel and Jules Iancu had returned to Bucharest in late 1921 and established an architectural firm. They designed many buildings. In fact, they changed the façade of Bucharest with cubistic and modernistic buildings. These were mostly blocks of flats, and some belonged to my grandparents, the Iancus. My grandmother had to sell most of these in order to bribe Lungianu and the police to save my father. The Iancu brothers belonged to the Romanian intelligentsia but as time went on, they were referred to as 'Jewish architects'. They realized that antisemitism was rife and rising. They traveled to Palestine, where they received special passports enabling them to leave Romania, and in 1941, they left together with their families for Palestine. My father George also wanted to emigrate, but my mother opposed it. She was not going to leave with a two-year-old child! Besides, she did not want to separate from her family. My father, despite my mother's objections, decided to join his brothers in Palestine.

The story goes that he left with only a rucksack on his back. But he took one look at the ship Struma and decided that it was not safe and returned home.

The Tragedy of the Struma

In December 1941, the only ship allowed to leave for Palestine was the Struma. The ship had been commissioned by the New Zionist Organization and the Irgun (Hebrew for the National Military Organization, an underground paramilitary group active during the British mandate of Palestine) and was the last ship to leave Europe in wartime. The ship was an old cargo barge used to carry cattle along the Danube and was suited for no more than 150 passengers. It left the port of Constanta in December 1941 with 769 people on board. The objective was to anchor in Turkey and from there to await certificates for Palestine from the British administration. The ship broke down several times on the way to Istanbul and it took three days to arrive. This distance is now traveled by ferry. The Turkish authorities prevented the passengers from disembarking for fear that they would remain there permanently, should the British authorities refuse certificates to enter Palestine. So, the ship remained in Istanbul for 70 days. There was an acute shortage of water and food on board despite help from the Jewish community of Istanbul.

The British refused to allow the ship to bring the refugees to Palestine and pressured the Turkish authorities to return the vessel to Romania, despite the fact the captain said that the ship was in no way able to return to Romania. On 23 February 1942, the Struma was towed back by the Turkish Police onto the Black Sea and abandoned. The next day, it was mistakenly torpedoed, apparently by a Russian submarine. There were 103 children on board. There was only one survivor! Sadly, my mother's instincts not to leave on the Struma were well-founded. And George, who was an engineer by profession, was ultimately right not to sail on it.

Chapter 2
Romania Is Liberated

April 1944 saw Bucharest bombed like never before. The bombings were by the Allied forces, and they kept coming. The Americans came in the morning and the British at night. Our street was heavily bombed. One night, the street was in flames. Our apartment was a mess. The door of our apartment had been ripped from its hinges and lay flat against our neighbor's door. The windows were shattered. Fortunately, none of us were hurt. In the midst of that devastation, my mother's brother Nelu arrived on his motorcycle to take me to Omama's apartment where it was thought safer for me to be. As a six-year-old child, I thought this was most exciting and I could only think of the motorcycle ride with Uncle Nelu.

The Allies advanced in France, and on 29 August 1944, the Russians entered Bucharest. Sebastian writes *all over the city people shouted with delight. Antonescu had been overthrown and a new government formed and an armistice accepted.* The Germans caught unawares, launched a bombing attack on the city. Without any warning, they bombed Bucharest for more than 60 hours. I remember this well. Our shelter was underneath one of the largest buildings in Bucharest, namely the head office of the National Insurance Company. It had several rooms, one of which sheltered a German general who had been taken prisoner. We children were very amused as he was fast asleep. He was tired and obviously relieved that the war was over for him.

On Thursday, 31 August, a parade of Soviet heavy tankers took place on the boulevard that once housed the Kimelman family, and where my mother grew up. Everybody was elated. We were free! The Allied forces, the United States and the British arrived in planes and quickly left. The Russians came on foot and remained.

Ion Antonescu was deposed on 23 August 1944. The Germans, who were still in Romania, attempted to seize Bucharest. Young Jewish men, among them Uncle Nelu, rushed to the only remaining airport, Beneasa, to prevent the German planes from taking off. There was a lot of fighting. You could hear it in Bucharest. Luckily, US bombs flattened the German planes. I remember coming out in the street, along with everybody else, and welcoming the little silver streamers the American planes showered us with.

We were occupied by the Soviet forces shortly afterwards. Slowly but surely, we became a satellite of the USSR. King Michael, who I surprisingly was to meet several times later, abdicated in 1947 and with his family left for England. Romania became a republic under one party, the Romanian communist Party.

Life Under the New Regime

Life under the communists was tough. My parents divorced in 1946 and my father moved with his mother to his sister's house and he subsequently in mid-1947 emigrated to Palestine. My grandmother Rachel phoned to tell me that he had left to join his brothers there.

I was terribly upset. As it happened, the British, in order to reduce emigration to Palestine, diverted his ship to Cyprus. He was held in Cyprus for six months.

In September 1946, I entered Grade 1 at Notre Dame de Zion School, my mother's old school. The medium of instruction was Romanian, although many of the nuns were French. Because my parents did not want me to be affected by the divorce, they decided that I should board. Big mistake! The first night, as a boarder, I cried for my mother all night. The next morning the nuns phoned my mother, "Rosica, come and fetch her," they said. I continued as a day student.

The Romanian intellectual elite was French speaking and French language teaching continued for a while. I had a tutor, who came to our little apartment to teach me French. However, in 1947, all Western influences in Romania ceased, as did the bicultural agreement with France. Russian was to be introduced as a second language in Romania. It was obligatory to teach it in schools. I admit that we did not take too seriously to our Russian teacher, to my regret many years later, when at Cornell University, I was keen to study Russian as part of my doctorate.

Also in 1947, Notre Dame de Zion School had closed down and the nuns were ordered to leave Romania. I had to change to a state school. My mother warned me not to mention that my parents were critical of Stalin or of the communists. There were informers all around and if reported, parents could be arrested. In my daily prayers, I asked God to keep my mouth shut if there were political discussions. And then, there were rations. My mother was one of a generation of pretty girls who did not study anything in particular and therefore did not qualify for work. The slogan was 'no work no food'. She decided to approach one of her former student tutors, a man called Neumann, who had served in Spain with the Republican forces and, on returning after the war to Bucharest, had established a large law firm. Neumann took pity on her and gave her a job. She was one of the assistants in the firm. Every morning she, along with everyone else in the office, was obliged to read and discuss the news in the communist newspaper *Scantaia,* (The Spark.) And at this point, she decided that the family should endeavor to leave Romania.

Meanwhile, my mother started seeing Tidy Calmi again. He hadn't married and he had waited for her to divorce George. My mother would often take me to visit him. He had a small apartment, and he would always have little presents for me hidden around the two rooms. He was very keen for me to continue learning the French language and one of my fondest memories is sitting on his lap while he taught me to sing the French National song, *La Marsellaise.* He was fluent in French, having spent much time as a student in Paris, but I later discovered that he was also fluent in German and English. I loved the French language and spent my afternoons away from school reading French classics. I enjoyed reading Alexander Dumas, Madame de Sevigny, Jules Verne, and others.

My family was not at all sporty, perhaps because they were so preoccupied with just surviving. Yet they recognized that gymnastics and ballet were important for a girl's development, and I shared a gym trainer with the little girl who lived upstairs from us. Olga was my best friend and classmate. Her father had been a famous newspaper editor, but when the communists came, he had to flee. The family who had been comfortable before, struggled without their father. It was sad and I felt for Olga as she remained behind when we left Romania. Many years later, Olga, now a pediatrician, was given permission to leave and established a practice in New York City.

My mother discussed emigration with Tidy and he suggested that my mother and I leave first. It was a good idea to apply, as my father was already in Israel, and reunification of families was accepted by Romanian authorities as a valid reason for exit permits. Tidy suggested that marrying my mother could wait until he too could exit Romania. Omama Marie never forgave him for this suggestion, although sensible in retrospect.

School was not difficult for me as I was a good student and learned easily. However, I was put out when a system was introduced that a good student should mentor a weak student. Today, this is called peer mentoring and it is a good idea, but in communist Romania, mentoring involved not just mentoring, but also splitting the marks with the partner. I really resented my partner, because she did not improve and my marks were pulled down, as a result.

The Pioneer Movement was an organization created by the Soviet Government shortly after the October Revolution. It was introduced in 1917. It was established in

Romania in 1949 and I did everything in my power to be selected and to be invested as a Pioneer before leaving the country. The purpose of the Pioneer Movement was to educate children to be loyal to the ideals of communism and to the communist party, as expressed in the motto "Pioneer be ready to fight for the cause of the communist Party." Being invested in the first Pioneer Movement in Romania was regarded as a great honor for a student and I greatly aspired to it. You were initiated by older pioneers, given a red scarf and a badge, followed by a salute. I desperately wanted and indeed succeeded in being invested with the first batch to be initiated. I took the scarf and the badge with me and kept them throughout our many moves around the world.

Chapter 3
Leaving Romania

In about 1948, my mother started applying to leave Romania. It was very difficult and the queues at the Ministry of Interior to apply for an exit permit (not a passport) were huge. My mother queued for many early mornings in the hope of seeing the director and submitting our application. One very early morning, she took me with her. I remember it well. After spending some time in the queue, we were ushered into the director's room. The director happened to have been one of my mother's tutors. Now, a highly placed communist, he headed this important position, where he literally decided the fate of countless Jewish people. He was also Jewish (his name was originally Hecht) but he was called Colonel Holban. He was a big man (or so it seemed to me.)

Holban recognized my mother but did not show any friendliness. He asked me why I wanted to leave I said that I wanted to join my father. He took in the application and said, "Don't have any illusions so that you are not disillusioned."

We returned home exhausted and dispirited. But the next day, we were informed that we had been given permission to leave! And so it was that in March 1950, shortly after my 12th birthday, we left Bucharest by train for Constanta. Omama Marie was allowed to leave with us. The passenger ship, Transylvania, was the only way one could exit Romania. The Joint Distribution Committee, together with the recently established Israeli government, covered the cost of the passage ($55 per passenger). So, some 47,000 Jewish people were able to leave Romania for Israel in 1950. Fortunately, this system of payments continued for the decade from 1950 to 1960, and eventually, all our family and friends were able to leave Romania. Naturally, the cost per head increased over this period!

The Trip

Preparations for leaving were feverish. One could only take a suitcase with one's personal items. No money or jewels were permitted. The paintings my mother had by Marcel Janco had to be left as they were for the next family, who was to occupy our apartment.

We went to say goodbye to Tidy and he gave me a gift, a tiny gold ring with a little diamond inside. My mother decided to let me keep it and to hide it in the ribbon of the hat I was going to wear on the way to Constanta. When my uncle Nelu heard of this, he was horrified. He said that it would imperil us. My mother decided to take the diamond out and give it to my aunt Dida to keep. The gold ring I kept in my coat pocket. I had a coat with large pockets of which the lining was broken. I decided to ensure that I would have enough pumpkin seeds for the trip and literally filled the bottom of my coat with the seeds. And so, I sailed through customs with my ring and my pumpkin seeds. The little diamond was not so lucky. When my aunt Dida and her family were allowed to leave Romania one year later, upon arriving in Constanta and seeing how difficult customs were and how thoroughly they searched, she threw the diamond in a bin.

The Journey to Israel

The train to Constanta was a regular passenger train but it left from the cattle station to keep it secret. Leaving the country was seen as a vote of no confidence in the communist regime and a bad example to other citizens. There were no lights at the station and so it was in darkness that we said goodbye to the family. I was crying, having to leave the rest of our family behind, especially my beloved aunt Dida, who was in hospital for a gallbladder operation.

I still recall that memory of our farewells. The image I had on leaving Bucharest was in dramatic contrast to when my husband Denis and I returned to the city in 1992, forty-two years later.

By way of explanation, South Africa had just opened diplomatic relations with Romania and the Foreign Minister, Pik Botha, invited me with Denis of course, he being one of the opposition Democratic Party and their Foreign Affairs leader to visit Romania as a goodwill gesture. "Anita," he said, "you must go to Romania." We were welcomed with a red carpet and a bouquet of red roses at the airport. But more about that later.

To return to the Transylvania experience, the ship was pleasant enough. My mother and I shared a small cabin, while Omama Marie was in another cabin. An incident occurred before the ship sailed. One of the passengers, came knocking on our door begging my mother to hide his wife's very expensive looking diamond ring. The Romanian authorities were searching the ship and without thinking of the possible consequences, my mother agreed to hide the ring. Fortunately, we were not searched, and my mother was able to return the ring to its owner. For years afterwards, she remembered that occurrence and marveled at how she could have put our lives at risk with this charitable act. We became friends with that family and later visited them in Kvar Saba where they chose to settle. Kvar Saba was a small town then. You could hear the jackals howling at night. Today, it is a thriving city.

I remember it because it gave me my first experience of walking in an orange grove, the scent of which is still with me today. Oranges were precious in Romania. One orange would last me a week, as I ate one segment a day.

Of course, Israel is today one of the leading producers of oranges in the world. My father knew that I loved them, which is why when he met us, as the ship docked in Haifa, his pockets were full of oranges.

Chapter 4
Life in Israel in 1950

My father found it very difficult to find a job in Haifa. Eventually, he found one as a railway engineer. He continued to live with his mother, Omama Rachel, who had preceded us to Israel. It was obvious that my parents were not to be reconciled. The first night we spent in Haifa was traumatic for me. It had only been five years since Jewish people had been liberated from the concentration camps and they were still talking about their experiences.

The owners of the little hotel we stayed in had been through the camps and they told us what they had endured. I listened feverishly and couldn't sleep the whole night. It was an experience I have not forgotten and for many years I would have nightmares about the Holocaust. We had been through the war, and antisemitism, but we had been fortunate not to be deported.

We left for Tel Aviv the following day and chose to stay in a little hotel named King Solomon Hotel. The hotel was a stone's throw from the sea. In fact, the seafront, Sfat HaYam, today a high-rise of luxury hotels, was in those days, a haven for the recently arrived immigrants. There were a number of little cafes where music blasted out every night and where young refugees who had survived the war, were exuberant, celebrating a promising new life. They would meet in the cafes, eat watermelon, drink tea and dream about the future.

We were fortunate to be able to afford a hotel, even though a cheap hotel. I think that my aunt Gisela sent us the money. Most immigrants in the early 1950s went first to Ma'abarots or transit camps. These were tent cities, with mud underfoot and supervised by Israeli camp police. Immigrants, who came in with no money, stayed in the transit camp with the promise of later receiving a house, a fridge and work. The new immigrants spent the day waiting in line to shower, to go to the lavatory, and for food. There was no privacy. Jews from Europe, especially those who had survived the Holocaust, were living close to Jews from the Middle East, Moroccans, Yemenites, and Persians. The Israeli authorities wanted to remove the Europeans from the camps as quickly as possible, which led to accusations of discrimination and racism. Barbed wire separated the camps from the rest of the surroundings, reminding the concentration camp survivors of what they endured during the Holocaust.

All new immigrants, who arrived in Israel came through the Port of Haifa and to Sha'ar Ha-'aliyah, the first absorption camp. People waited for several days to be sorted to go to other camps. One year after we arrived in Israel, my aunt Dida arrived with her husband Marcel, and their young son Michael. A few days before arriving, Marcel had sent us a telegram in French, "Reservez meilleur bet olim" ("Please reserve best transit camp.") This caused much amusement among our family and friends.

I traveled with Marcel's brother and sister-in-law to Haifa to receive them. Needless to say, we were not allowed near the ship but were sent to Sha'ar Ha-'aliyah to see them. I recall waiting in front of the barbed wire and Dida eventually arriving, in a disheveled state, and with tears in her eyes saying, "Get us out of here, please." She had queued for hours for the bathroom and for food. They had heard Moroccans fighting in the adjacent tent. Fortunately, they got out within a few days and came to our hotel in Tel Aviv. Work was hard to find, and people did whatever they could.

So, Marcel became the night porter in our hotel. Marcel had owned a textile factory before the arrival of the communists, and his factory was nationalized in 1947. He was asked to take his coat and umbrella and leave! It was the end of his factory. My mother learned to darn nylon stockings and she mended her customer's stockings in our little hotel room.

Life for Me in Tel Aviv Was Exciting

I teamed up with two other young Romanians, Odette, and Colette. The three of us saved money by delivering flowers around Tel Aviv on Friday evenings, before Shabbat. This was a wonderful custom and it continues to this day to send flowers to one's wife or mother before Shabbat, the holy day in Israel. The three of us would split the tips. It was not a great business. We kept the money while our parents had to replace our sandals, destroyed by walking the streets of Tel Aviv. Our entrepreneurial spirit was rewarded with an article in the Romanian newspaper in

Tel Aviv. Odette did not remain long in Tel Aviv. The family had relatives in Brazil and soon left for Rio.

Colette and I had to go to school despite not having any Hebrew. For a couple of days, we attended a Tel Aviv school, but we agreed the type of schooling was too unstructured for us. We were used to more conventional schooling. Colette and I developed a lifelong friendship—she remained in Israel and became a top-level Israeli diplomat and politician.

One day I went to visit my uncle Marcel Janco. He was living in Tel Aviv with his wife and daughter, Dadi. Years later, on an evening visit, Dadi Janco gave me some lithographs of her father, which today grace the lounge in our Cape Town home.

School in Jaffa

My mother and Colette's parents decided to send us to Pensionnat St. Joseph an old school in Jaffa run by nuns. The medium of the school was French and it was attended by children from various embassies, Arab as well as Jewish children. Although most of our teachers were nuns, we also had lay teachers. We were particularly impressed with our Hebrew teacher, ironically a beautiful young Palestinian girl. We got to know her well and my sympathy for women of the Middle East derived from the time I attended the school. At both Cornell University, as well as in London, I enjoyed the company of many such intelligent and sensitive women. The school is still standing today, but the very old hospital opposite the school, which used to house the nuns, is now a luxury hotel.

Colette and I preferred to be boarders but after a few weeks, we came home, and our parents agreed to allow us to be day students and travel to Jaffa from our hotel in Tel Aviv. Today, Tel Aviv and Jaffa are one city, Tel Aviv-Yafo. You can reach Jaffa from Tel Aviv within ten minutes by car. In 1950, we had to travel by bus over desolate land. We would often see soldiers doing maneuvers on that road. Jaffa is the ancient port city inhabited for centuries by Arab traders. In May 1948, after Israel's Declaration of Independence, most of the Palestinian population of Jaffa fled. Jaffa's ancient alleyways and streets were populated by Jewish refugees such as one of my uncle Nelu's brothers-in-law, a famous jeweler from Bucharest. He had a studio in the courtyard of one of these abandoned houses. I went to see him, and he agreed to replace the small diamond in the ring Tidy gave me before our departure. He replaced the diamond with a little ruby.

Years later, when I attended a conference in Jerusalem, upon visiting the art and jewelry galleries in Mamilla Mall in front of Jaffa Gate, I saw a bangle that I liked. I returned to Cape Town and described it to a jeweler. She melted all the jewels I had received from my parents, including the little ring, into an exact copy of the bangle I had seen in Jerusalem. I wear it every day.

In 1950, food was scarce in Israel, and meat was rationed. There was no milk and most oranges had worms in them; good oranges were exported for much-needed foreign exchange. Yet the mood was buoyant and there were many tourists, mainly Americans. It seemed that many of them were looking for young girls to marry. Indeed, there were many divorcees and widows around and they all dreamed of meeting a 'Mr. Rockefeller'. My mother was financially very insecure. She had to provide for my grandmother and me. We were living in one room in the hotel, with my grandmother cooking our meals on a small electric stove. The toilet and the shower were down the corridor.

No one had told me how my mother met her 'Mr. Rockefeller' but she met an American and became engaged. He was from New York City and owned a dry-cleaning business. He was in the process of divorcing his wife. He gave my mother a beautiful gold necklace and she gave him a photo of herself wearing it. A copy of the photo has been in my lounge all these years. I think she looks very happy.

The gentleman in question, I don't remember his name, suggested that we come to New York City via Havana because the United States still had an immigration quota. US immigrants were allowed entry to the United States through a national origin system. As we were stateless people without passports, our country of origin was considered to be Israel and Israel had a large number of applicants for the United States. It was therefore thought that it would be easier and faster to reach the United States through Cuba.

With my nanny in the park. German soldiers asked permission to
photograph me to send to Berlin, "a blond baby in Bucharest"

With my mother in the Iancu house

In the garden, made reference by Sandquist. From the earliest times, I associate the garden with anxiety communicated by the adults in the house

Once again in my grandparents garden

My Father George Iancu

My Aunt Gisela Chinigo

Marcel Janco's picture on the wall at Cabaret Voltaire

Tidy with Sonia in Paris, before the war.

With my mother, my grandmother Omama and Auntie Rosita
shortly after the war.

My mother in Tel Aviv. On her engagement to the American
fellow, who brought us to Havana.

With Colette and Odette. We delivered flowers all over Tel Aviv
on foot on Friday nights.

In Montréal, with Harry, my mother, Omama and my aunt, Dida.

Graduating from McGill University, in Montréal.

My Iraqi friend and neighbour at Cornell University.

Denis, when I met him at Cornell.

Farewell party in Montreal.

Chapter 5
We Fly to Havana

We left Tel Aviv at the beginning of 1952 by air for Havana. The trip was going to take several stops and at least four days. We went by BOAC, the forerunner of British Airways. The first stop was London, where we spent two days. While my mother was sleeping, I decided to visit London and I took a double-decker bus through the city. I loved what I saw. My mother was very upset with me to have gone without her permission.

The next leg of our trip was Paris. We went on an afternoon plane, full of elegant ladies going to Paris to shop. It was very civilized. We were offered champagne and petit fours. (Gone are those days!) My mother and I were most impressed. We did not stay in Paris, but took the plane to Nassau, via the Azores. We stayed a night in Nassau in a beautiful hotel. The next day, we flew into Havana to be met by mother's fiancé, who had made all this possible. We first stayed in a beach hotel in Havana.

Sojourn in Havana

A few days later, he arranged for us to stay in a boarding house in Vedado. Vedado is a popular part of Havana, it was full of beautiful colonial mansions. Some of these had been converted into boarding houses. Our boarding house included full board and many Cuban families chose to reside there with their children. Opposite our house was a beautiful white house. It looked palatial. The story was that the deposed Romanian King Carol II had stayed there with his Jewish wife, the former Elena Lupescu. The owner and resident of the mansion was an old lady, who lived there with what seemed to be an army of servants. From our house across the street, my mother and I often watched how the car would pull up at the entrance of the mansion and four or five servants would help the lady of the house into the car. Apart from the chauffeur, one servant would hold her handbag, another her umbrella and a third would open the car door to settle her into the car. My mother could not help herself from commenting that the scene was no longer suited for the second half of the twentieth century. After all, she had experienced communism and had seen how this had leveled the society from which she came. The scene was even more in contrast with that of the family, virtually around the corner, who was taking in laundry to wash.

We had arrived at just the time Fulgencio Batista established himself as dictator of Cuba. They say that before Castro's Revolution, Cuba was one of the most advanced and successful countries in Latin America. Fueled by the sale of sugar to the United States, the economy had grown dramatically. Although there were many poor people, there was a thriving middle and professional class.

In the boarding house, we met lawyers, doctors and engineers, and their families. They were extraordinarily friendly to us even though my mother battled to learn to speak Spanish. Because there were children of my age in the boarding house, I learned Spanish very quickly. Romanian is a Latin language, which is of course my mother tongue, and I spoke French as well, which I learned in Bucharest and Israel, so Spanish came easily to me.

I loved the soup made from black beans (frijoles negros), the plantain chips, and the fried bananas. Because of the sub-tropical climate, Havana has a lot of ants. It was not surprising to see an ant floating in the soup. My mother had a horror of insects floating in the soup. Incensed, she called the waiter and pointed to her soup, "Mira, un mosquito!" (In her excitement she used the word mosquito because it approximates the word *musca* which in Romania means a fly.) The waiter was insulted. "Señora, no es un mosquito, es una hormiga." ("Lady, this is not a mosquito, it is an ant!")

The boarding house was two streets away from the Malecon, the broad seawall that stretches for eight kilometers along the coast of Havana. We often went to the Malecon in the evenings. There was music and we loved to hear the call of the peanut seller, 'Mani' (peanuts), while he sang the song of the same name. Music is part of life in Havana, and I learned and loved the beautiful love songs of those days like Granada, Adios Amigos Compagneros de mi Vida, la Cucaracha and so many more! Cubans were very conservative. A girl had to be chaperoned to go out on a date. One beautiful girl who lived with her mother in the boarding house had a date. I remember that she was smartly dressed for the occasion, but the couple was to be accompanied by a bored elderly cousin. My friends and I were on the lookout for when she returned. The poor girl arrived home early. The date had been a disaster! They had hardly managed to talk to each other!

Stranded in Havana

Shortly after we arrived in Havana, my mother was dealt a devastating blow. Her fiancé had just had a stroke in New York City and decided not to divorce. We were literally stranded in Havana. My mother started giving French lessons to supplement our income.

In those days, telephone calls between countries were very difficult but I recall my mother receiving a phone call from her sister, Gisela, in Rome. She was concerned about my mother and promised to help to support us while we were in Havana. Sadly, Gisela was very ill. She died of ovarian cancer in July 1952 about the time Evita Perron died in Argentina. I recall the date because Evita's death was a very significant and sad occasion in Havana.

I Make a Big Discovery

In the meantime, it was obvious that we would have to leave Havana. Tidy lived in Israel. He had managed to leave Bucharest and he was in an Ulpan school for the intensive study of Hebrew. He corresponded regularly with my mother, and I sometimes read his letters, something which I was strictly not allowed to do. But one day, as my mother was out, I came upon a letter in which Tidy encouraged my mother 'to tell her the truth'. I gathered from the letter that he wanted my mother to tell me that he was my real father. Tidy had always been part of my life and I admired and respected him. He was an attractive figure and many times while reading a romantic book, I would often imagine the character looking like him. He never disciplined me, although I remember that before going on our visits, my mother would warn me to behave, so I assume I was misbehaving on some of those visits.

Tidy had always been good to me, played with me, taught me French, and paid me lots of attention, even though my mother always said that he had never offered to support me. My Omama Marie did not have much time for him and always said that he was very selfish. Perhaps so, but when in Havana I discovered this letter and confronted my mother with the finding, she denied the fact that Tidy was my father, as she had denied it all her life. The problem has been that I looked very much like him and as does my youngest son. Tidy had wished that we return to Israel, and to marry my mother.

In the meantime, my Omama Marie, my aunt Dida and her family had arrived in Canada. My uncle Marcel had a brother who had preceded the family to Montréal and he brought out the rest of the family. When my mother asked me where I wanted to go, I said immediately that I wanted to join my Omama and the rest of the family in Montréal. My mother agreed and so did Tidy, who undertook to immigrate to Canada. Uncle Marcel started the process of obtaining papers for Tidy to immigrate to Canada. It was a long process, and in the meantime, I was advised that I needed to go to school in Havana.

School in Havana

Our Cuban friends suggested that we approach the Dominicas Francesas College, a beautiful school run by nuns, not far from our boarding house. The nuns accepted me warmly into grade five, the year before the Ingreso al Bachillerato, the year that prepares you for high school. Of course, the language of instruction of the school was Spanish. This time, I had to sit for exams in Spanish. I adjusted to the language and even received a medal for my efforts. But I found the names of the many mountains of Cuba very difficult to recall! The experience of waking up very early in the morning to study was a good experience for me, an experience I put to good use years later when I had to study for the matriculation exams in English, and much later, Afrikaans.

In August 1952, we received our papers for immigration to Canada. In the six months that we spent in Havana, we had made many friends and we were very sad to leave them. They showered me with gifts that I still have with me today.

Chapter 6
On the Way to Montréal

Our flight to Montréal had to be via Miami. When we arrived in Miami, the customs official looked at the exit paper my mother handed him (remember, it was not a passport; it was simply a permission to leave Romania, written in Romanian). I remember the officer, while chewing gum, looked at the paper and shaking it, asked "What is this?"

Furthermore, our visa that was required to fly through the USA was valid for three weeks, whereas it had to be valid for six months.

No amount of pleading was to change the official's mind. He decreed that we should return to Havana. And so, we were put on a plane back to Havana. The problem was that our Cuban visa had expired the moment we left Havana. My mother was desperate. She telephoned one of her Cuban friends and asked him to meet us at the airport in Havana.

It was late when we arrived in Havana. In the middle of the night, we were transferred by police boat to Triscornia, an internment island for refugees like Ellis Island outside New York. Her friend accompanied us to the island in the police boat and returned to Havana, promising to do everything in his power to release us as soon as possible. We were assigned a room, more like a cell, with two camp beds and a side table between us. Mosquitoes plagued us all night. The next morning, we met some of our fellow internees. Some of them had been there for months and saw no way of being able to get their papers and leave.

My mother started phoning all our friends. A well-known lawyer, the father of one of my friends, succeeded in obtaining a release for us after three days. We returned to Havana for my mother to obtain an extension of the US visa. I was invited to spend the time with friends in a beach cottage outside Havana, while my mother was working on getting the visa. I remember that it was called Playa Hollywood (Hollywood Beach). Googling this beach today, it looks beautiful. I recall that my friends wanted to teach me to ride a bike! This had not been considered a necessity so far! I doubt that my mother had ever learned to ride a bike! (My sons are not impressed!)

On 26 August 1952, we finally arrived in Montréal. The trip was not without emotion. As the plane stopped in Washington, we saw the pilot and the stewardess looking at our papers. With more goodwill and more understanding, they allowed us to fly over US airspace on the way to Montréal. We had finally arrived to be with our family. Montréal would be my home for the following thirteen years.

Chapter 7
Montréal

My mother's family was very close. The center of my family was my grandmother, Omama. She had lived with us for most of my childhood. I was also close to my aunt Dida and her son Michael who was a few years younger than me. Nelu and his family were only to arrive in Montréal eight years later. He and his wife, Rosica had one son, Radu.

Because of the war and its aftermath, my parent's generation chose to have only one child each. Because of this, we were only three first cousins in my mother's family and we were very close. I was fortunate to be loved and protected by all. Despite my insecurities, particularly evidenced in Havana, where I was loath to let my mother out of my sight (with tantrums when she wanted to go out), the love of my family supported me throughout.

My family is Jewish, but not wholly religious. We always regarded being Jewish as being part of a culture, and our celebrations as being part of a 'cherished heritage' as the Israeli author Amos Oz writes. We observed the high holidays, and we were always together at those times.

I will always miss my family get-togethers and the delicious cooking prepared by Omama. She was a great cook and although not observant of recipes, she made wonderful Jewish and Romanian dishes. On leaving Romania, my grandmother had taken with her a cookery book by Sanda Marin.[4]

When I left for South Africa to be married, Omama gave it to me. I still have it. Aside from other dishes, it is full of the most delicious cakes, some of which I have successfully tried.

Our arrival in Montréal was a very happy one. I was delighted to be reunited with Omama, who immediately moved in with us. Dida and her family were not too far away. We moved to a 'rooming house' close to the center of Montréal. It had one big room, with Omama once again cooking on a little stove in the corner of the room. It did not have a private bathroom of course. The important thing was that we were together. My uncle Marcel began to apply for Tidy to join us.

Montréal High School for Girls

September is the month when schools start in North America, and I needed to go to school. My uncle explained that in Montréal, there were two school boards, the Catholic School Board which looked after the French Schools, and the Protestant School Board which looked after the English Schools. "You have to choose one or the other," he said. He recommended that I go to an English medium school, 'seeing that we are part of North America'. So, I was enrolled into Montréal High School for Girls, a few blocks from where we lived. This was established in 1875, the first high school for girls in the city, and it became a separate division of the Montréal High School, originally only for boys.

Originally the girls' school had its own lady principal and four teachers. It continued to exist in a shared building with the boys until 1965 when for the first time, boys and girls were united in one school. The school was housed in a beautiful building designed by leading Canadians who also designed the Montréal Museum of Arts.

I was enrolled in grade six, the first year of high school. There were two other immigrant girls in my class, one from what was then Yugoslavia, Dina; the other from Hungary. Dina and I became good friends and spoke French to one another. Six months later, without even realizing it, we switched to English and never looked back. I marvel at a child's resilience and ability to acquire and function in different languages. Not surprisingly, this became the center of my professional interest.

We had left Romania in March 1950, where I attended school in Romanian. The same year, I attended a French school for almost one and a half years. This was followed by Havana, where I attended a Spanish school for about six months, and finally, Montréal, where I had to learn in English. This makes four languages in the space of three years! The start of my schooling in Montréal coincided with the excitement of Queen Elizabeth II coronation. To celebrate it, the girls in our class were asked to prepare a scrapbook of the young royal family. I took that assignment very seriously.

In my aunt's apartment block, someone discarded their copies of the *London Illustrated News*, the weekly illustrated magazine. Naturally, it was full of pictures of the royal family. I would regularly go into the waste disposal room to retrieve the copies, search for photos of the royal family and place them in my scrapbook. I can still recall some of the photos seventy years later, particularly poignant as the Queen was recently celebrating her Platinum Jubilee. My scrapbook was a great success.

Living in Montréal

Montréal was a very divided city. The Jewish community belonged to the English side of Montréal. As children, we did not meet French children to play with. Although the French language was an essential part of the curriculum, we did not speak French to each other. As a city, Montréal was quite bland. There was only one venue for concerts, hockey, or other sports activities. That was the Forum.

My uncle Marcel's brother, who had facilitated the family's immigration to Canada moved away. He and his wife were bored in Montréal and yearned for Paris. Eventually, they moved to Toronto. Hungarian immigration, as a result of the Hungarian Revolution of 1956, changed Montréal for the better. Suddenly, you could drink good coffee in a cafe and enjoy a Vienna schnitzel in a small restaurant. Montréal is today one of the most cosmopolitan and exciting cities but it began with the Hungarian Revolution in 1956!

While I settled into our life in Montréal and found school and English reasonably easy, my mother struggled to provide for the three of us. During the long summer holidays, many Canadian children went to camp, but I did not go. Instead, I worked. My first job was as a salesgirl. The following year, I was employed by Simpson's Department Store in the complaints department. Having to listen to people's complaints from early morning was hardly inspiring. Neither was the next job with a stockbroker firm where I wrote out figures that came out of the machine on a blackboard.

For some reason, Tidy's permit to immigrate to Canada was taking a long time. He had graduated from Hebrew school and had a good job. He traveled to Paris to see his and my mother's old friends, Dr. Bibi and Sonia Ludmer, and sent my mother a bottle of perfume. My mother in turn repaired stockings and was struggling financially. I felt for her.

And that summer of 1954, while I was working for the stockbroker, I decided that my mother needed to find a husband. I came home one evening and told my mother that she should go for a weekend to Ste Agathe, the village in the Laurentian Mountains, where hotels often entertained Jewish men and women looking for partners. My mother took the weekend off, traveled to Ste Agathe and returned with a fiancé! Harry was divorced, was of Romanian descent, had two grown-up sons, and owned a factory for men's trousers. And he proved to be a fine gentleman, very suitable to be my mother's husband.

Our New Life

My mother married Harry in 1954, two years after arriving in Montréal. He agreed that my Omama and I should live with them. He bought a beautiful house for my mother in the lovely suburb of Town of Mount Royal. For the first time in my life, I had my own room. Many houses in Montréal have basements converted for parties and games rooms. Our basement was organized for parties. It was inviting and spacious.

My mother and Harry traveled around Canada and the USA and had many friends. Montréal has a large Romanian community from Bucharest.

In fact, there was an understanding that while traveling on a bus, you should refrain from speaking freely in Romanian lest you be understood by others in the bus. My mother and Harry entertained a great deal. Omama did most of the cooking and was famous for the quality and spread of her buffets.

For some reason, I did not want Romanian friends. My friends came from many different countries and we spoke English when together. Like other teenagers, we had parties, especially sweet sixteen parties. At one of these parties, I met Danny. He was in the first year of Chemical Engineering at McGill University. I was only in grade 10 and I had another year to go before matriculating. Although living in the Town of Mount Royal was far from my high school, I continued to attend it. Every day, I had to take a bus and a train to reach my school and to return home. I was a good student and received a bursary every year while in high school.

My mother bought my clothes and gave me the pocket money I needed. Omama discovered that she enjoyed television. She loved watching the wrestling shows and we often watched The Ed Sullivan show on Sunday nights. A couple of times, we spent New Year's Eve together watching the festivities at the Waldorf Astoria Hotel with the Guy Lombardo orchestra. That is until I went out on New Year's Eve myself. I saw Danny every day for about one year. However, I was immature and naive and he began to see other girls. It was quite a blow to me, and I took a long time to get over him. Danny's best friend was Peter, another engineering student. We introduced my friend Dina to Peter and they remained together and married shortly after Peter's graduation. He was offered a place at Cornell University to do a PhD in Engineering, and shortly after they were married and moved to Ithaca.

This was to influence the course of my life, as it was because of this I applied to Cornell University for post-graduate work. But coming back to my matric year, the year Danny and I split up, was a difficult year for me. I immersed myself in my studies, with excellent results. I received the highest overall marks for my school, earned the Governor General Silver Medal for Overall Proficiency, the Bronze Medal for Latin, and a McGill University Scholarship.

McGill University

McGill University is well known throughout the world. It has a stellar faculty and to be an accepted student you had to have high marks.

The psychology department is one of the best in the world. The late Professor Donald Hebb at the time the head of the department of psychology deserves his position as arguably, the father of modern neuropsychology.[5] Having worked with the celebrated Professor Wilder Penfield at the Montréal Neurological Hospital, he expounded a theory of learning, which is widely accepted today.

He maintained that learning happens when brain cells (neurons) repeatedly occur together. It must be remembered this was the time, where behaviorism in psychology was at its highest. Hebb was a cognitive psychologist totally opposed to behaviorism.

I decided to study psychology and enrolled in the BA honors psychology course, whose mentor was Donald Hebb. Hebb was an intimidating fellow but also had a wicked sense of humor. In one of his introductory lectures in psychology attended by over 200 students, he lectured on the issue of nature versus nurture. "Nature is most important," he said, "so, ladies and gentlemen, it is all in your jeans." (genes) to the howling of the students. Hebb was to become the Chancellor of McGill University in the early 70s.

Another illustrious member of staff, Professor Wally Lambert, a social psychologist, was commencing his now famous research on bilingualism in the same department. He believed that if you immerse a child from early on in a second language situation, it will have positive cognitive and social benefits to the child.[6]

This started the well-known immersion research in Montréal. Multilingual myself, I was interested in the consequences of early bilingual exposure in childhood and this was to influence both my Master and my PhD dissertations. Montréal is a very bilingual city but during my time living there, the French and the English populations did not mix. While studying psychology, I continued my interest in French and Spanish literatures and I attended these classes regularly.

Seated behind me was one of the few French Canadian students at McGill. I thought he was good looking and charming and we flirted regularly across benches.

One evening, to my surprise, he phoned to ask me to the ball held every year by the engineering students, the Plumbers Ball. I was dumbfounded. I wanted to go but I was scared of what my friends would say if I went out with a French Canadian. I declined, giving an inane excuse. I have never forgiven myself for this.

Montréal society was very parochial. Jews went out with Jews, Catholics with Catholics, French Canadians with French Canadians, and so on. It took a later cohort of immigrants to break this lockjaw. In the early 1960s when my mother's cousins, both doctors, arrived from Bucharest, they worked and taught in French hospitals.

Our honors course in psychology was over the course of three years. It was a small class and being together for all that time, we struck many and long-lasting friendships. One of my fellow students and lifelong friend became famous after an article she wrote in Lancet about her research on Einstein's brain. She is today a fellow of the Royal Society of Canada.

When it was time for graduate work, we received graduate assistantships, which were enough to cover our rent and our expenses. Tuition was paid by the university. This is how fortunate we had been in the 1950s and 1960s! My entire education, including my graduate studies did not cost my mother a penny! She only helped me to pay for the phone calls to Montréal.

Chapter 8
Cornell University

I had applied to a number of universities for my graduate studies and had received offers from Purdue University in Indiana, the University of Michigan at Ann Arbor and Cornell University in Ithaca, New York. I opted for the latter as I had already visited the campus while Dina and Peter were there and was very impressed. It was also closer to Montréal and its psychology department had an excellent reputation. The professor of social psychology, WW Lambert was Professor Wally Lambert's brother, who had been my promoter at McGill. I was offered a research assistantship in the Department of Child Development, now the College of Human Ecology.

Cornell University is one of the eight Ivy League (private) universities in the United States. It is set among beautiful gardens, waterfalls, and gorges. It has a beautiful campus overlooking the city of Ithaca and Cayuga Lake and prides itself on its academic excellence and is indeed viewed as one of the most prestigious universities in the world. My promoter that first year was Urie Bronfenbrenner, a prolific researcher, founder of the field of human ecology, and of the Peace Corps Project. He was a very popular lecturer, when he was available! A native speaker of Russian, the detente between the Soviet Union and the West gave him the opportunity to travel to Russia to research and compare the child-rearing practice in the USSR, in the Israel kibbutz, and in the USA. Needless to say, he was very busy! Upon arriving at Cornell, aside from my research work for the department, I was intrigued by all the university could offer. My ambition was to study Russian so that I could read Russian literature in its original language.

I had just missed Vladimir Nabokov, the author of *Lolita*, who had been a very popular professor of Russian literature for a number of years. I also continued attending courses in French and Spanish literature. To this, I added a superb course on the history of art!

Needless to say, I gorged myself in wonderful courses but not for long as I had to devote myself to my studies. I decided to change my promoter.

Professor Harry Levin was teaching language development, a new field of study. I found it fascinating and it fitted in well with my interest in bilingual research. Levin was involved, along with the Psychology Department at Harvard University on Project Literacy.[7]

It was one of the first projects looking at literacy, as part of language. My interest in literacy was sparked at that time by Levin. He was a wonderful man, always interested in his students and very generous in his approach. Seeing my interest in the development of language in children, he invited me to be his teaching assistant.

Social Life at Cornell

Leaving Montréal and the stifling atmosphere of the late 1950s was liberating. My friend and colleague, Esther, a practicing Jew who was also accepted at Cornell University and I found our wings.

We were to meet many students from all over the world. A quarter of the graduate students at Cornell are presently foreign, and no doubt, the same proportion applied in our time. The foreign students were and are selected from the best of their countries. We met the charismatic Spanish students in the Architecture Faculty, and Iraqi and Lebanese students, who were our neighbors. Saddam Hussein, for all his failings, spent lavishly on sending students to study in the USA. One of our very best friends was an Iraqi, Salwa. She was already a PhD student and in her apartment we argued through the night over the Palestinian question. Sadly, one of the students died young after he returned to Beirut as assistant to the famous Lebanese entrepreneur and politician Emil Bustani. They died together in an air crash.

We also met our first Russian student. He was tall, handsome with a heavy Russian accent! He was very popular among the graduate students but we suspected that he was a spy!

I obtained my MA in mid-1962 and returned to Montréal. I was appointed a researcher in the McGill Department of Psychology to work with Canadian veterans and study their response to various drugs. I was stationed at the Montréal Veterans Hospital and lived at home. Not a great idea after the freedom I had at Cornell! The research did not amount to much as some of the promised drugs never arrived! One of my friends from Cornell, having completed her PhD, was appointed to the McGill Department of Psychology. One Sunday, she invited me to meet a fellow student from Cornell, who was visiting Montréal. He was a PhD student in the Department of Mechanical Engineering, an Ismaili from East Africa. He was very attractive and I saw him a lot when I returned to Cornell and to a teaching assistantship with Professor Harry Levin.

The American PhD requires preparation for a content exam and a dissertation. My major field was child development, with two minor fields of social psychology, and what is today neuropsychology. I prepared for those three subjects, as well as Russian for a graduate exam. The PhD requires some understanding of two additional languages. It is not required that you speak the languages but it is important that you are able to read the language.

I had already written and passed the French exam. Now, I had to do the Russian, which required a great deal of preparation.

In January 1964, at a party of one of our friends, I spotted a young man, sitting at the other end of the room. He was blond, blue-eyed, speaking energetically to some of my friends. He was wearing a cravat, so I thought he would be a foreign student. As I expected to know most of the guests, I asked Linda, whose party it was, who was the young man. She said Denis Worrall. "That is Denis Worrall?" I asked. I had heard about Denis Worrall, a doctoral student in the Department of Political Science. He was South African and known to give lectures on the future of South Africa. Not apologetic for South Africa, he argued that South Africa would change and he proposed a federal system not unlike Nigeria, from where he had just returned, after having spent a year at the University of Ibadan. Denis was very different! Firstly, he sported an English accent, which makes one stand out at an American university. He was also very charming. His date was a French girl and my date and I gave them a lift home, promising that we would be in touch. Of course, Abby my date, an Ismaili East African, could hardly approve of Denis!

My romance with Abby was beginning to fade. There were too many cultural differences between us. I began to see Denis. But shortly after meeting Denis, Esther and I had to return to Montréal for the funeral of our much-loved friend June, who had died in a fire, while she was studying for her PhD at the University of Austin Texas. June was 25 years old and my best friend since high school.

Chapter 9
Romance with Denis

Returning to Ithaca, I began seeing Denis more regularly. However, he was due to travel to California for a summer teaching post at UCLA, whereas I spent the summer in Ithaca preparing for exams. In September, when he returned, our romance took a more serious turn. He was finishing his doctoral dissertation and was a teaching assistant in his department. Although he had the reputation of being somewhat of a ladies' man, he persuaded me that this was not his nature. He began to write his thesis from my apartment. On one of his trips to New York City, he bought a cookery book for me. It was by Mr. Diat, the celebrated chef of the Ritz Hotel! He had high hopes for me, who had never cooked before!

Our relationship was going from strength to strength. We were very good companions and we were living in ideal conditions. I was studying for my exams, while assisting Professor Harry Levin in his course on language development. Denis was writing his dissertation on Nigerian Federation.

Meanwhile, the personal news from Montréal was worrying. My mother's husband, Harry had been diagnosed with cerebral arterial sclerosis. He lost his factory. My mother saw that she needed to earn their living and she decided to go to Paris to learn how to be a cosmetician. She spent three months in Paris studying at the Payot Institute. In October, on her way home, I asked her to come via Ithaca. I wanted her to meet Denis. I can still see the scene when Denis welcomed her as she descended from the Greyhound bus from New York. He was very charming and they hit it off immediately. That evening, I gave a party for friends and professors to meet her. It was a very successful party and my mother, who had guessed that Denis was very special to me, said afterwards, "You can go out with Clark Gable but it does not mean that you have to marry him." She wanted to shield me from what she thought was going to be a disappointment.

Denis was hard working and ambitious. He was passionate about his country, South Africa. Furthermore, he was not only good looking but also the perfect gentleman. I found him so different to the other students and so stimulating. I was very comfortable in his presence and he made me feel confident. Not thinking, I said to one of my friends, "He makes me feel so confident that I could even meet the Queen of England in his presence." Prescient words! I don't know why these words popped into my mouth.

We were in love, but sadly his time at Cornell was coming to a close. In February 1965, he handed in his dissertation and was planning to return to South Africa. He had received an appointment as senior lecturer in political science at the University of Natal, Durban. On the way home, he planned to stop over in Vienna to visit an old girlfriend he had befriended in Nigeria. She was the daughter of the Austrian Ambassador to Nigeria and Denis had become close to the family. I decided to go back to Montréal for a visit. We flew on the same flight to New York, where we were to say goodbye. The visit to New York made us both realize that we were closer to each other than we thought.

Denis had been a foreign student on a Fulbright scholarship. As a Cornell fellow, he was given the opportunity to study in Nigeria. In those days, South Africans were persona non grata in the rest of Africa. Yet he had been received with open arms as a Cornell fellow by the University of Ibadan.

Many years later, Sir Sonny Ramphal, Secretary General of the Commonwealth, hosted a lunch in honor of the Eminent Persons Group (EPG), about to the visit the imprisoned Mandela in South Africa. Denis was invited as ambassador for South Africa and I was invited with him.

General Obasanjo, former President of Nigeria, hugged me and told me admiringly, "Your husband was the winner of the one mile in the annual athletic championship between Nigeria and Ghana universities." Denis had loved his stay in Nigeria.

As a foreign student in political science, Denis had the opportunity to meet many American politicians, among others President John Kennedy and the future President Lyndon Johnson. The latter's civil rights stance impressed Denis (our second son is named Lyndon). As a student in the USA, he wrote numerous articles, especially for the

Cornell *Trojan Horse*, a student newspaper but with a very important readership. He was acutely aware of his country's problems and always searched for workable solutions.

While a graduate student, he corresponded with the South African Foreign Minister, Dr. Hilgard Muller, and a former Rhodes Scholar, who it seems was also searching for answers. In a letter, Dr. Muller thanked Denis for the interesting and useful suggestions made in one of Denis' articles. He wrote, "I found several of the thoughts you develop very stimulating. My own experience has been that local politics need not be an obstacle to the approaches you suggest, because the South African electorate is more realistic and advanced in their views than people realize." Dr. Muller had made a similar point in a speech he delivered while he was ambassador to London a few years before. It was also a prescient statement, which President FW de Klerk later pursued in a referendum on majority rule which white South Africans voted a resounding 'yes' to. Denis also experienced this in 1987, after he had resigned from his post as ambassador in London, as a protest at the slow pace of change and stood as an independent in the Helderberg election dramatically to lose by only 39 votes out of 18,000 cast.

Denis always quoted the great twentieth-century historian Arnold Toynbee who once said, "South Africa is important to the whole world—because if it can find answers as to how the different races, languages and religions can live together in peace, nobody in the world with similar problems can claim to fail." He set his life's goal in this statement and must have quoted it in hundreds of speeches and articles.

We Say Goodbye

The day before we said goodbye in New York, Denis had lunch with Lord Caradan, the UK permanent representative to the UN, while I spent the day at the Metropolitan Museum of Art. Our stay in New York was short. We realized that we were fonder of each other than we thought. The next day, we parted—I to Montréal and Denis to South Africa, via Vienna. It was with a heavy heart that I flew to Montréal that day. I remember that on the plane I heard President Lyndon Johnson had ordered an increase in US military forces in Vietnam, from what were at the time 75,000 to 150,000 troops. Everyone was shocked. It was the escalation in the war.

In Montréal, my mother was forced to sell her house in the Town of Mount Royal. She, with Harry and Omama had to move to a rented flat. I was concerned about them as once again my mother had to fend for her family.

An Airletter Romance

I returned to Ithaca to concentrate on my A level exams. Denis had returned to South Africa and had gone straight to Durban to take up his post at the university and kept his word to me to write regularly. He had been invited to do a weekly public affairs column for the *Sunday Tribune*, Durban's Sunday newspaper. And quickly acquired a national readership. We had to satisfy ourselves with airletters. Telephoning from South Africa to the USA was rare. In April, in the short university vacation, when he visited his family in Gordons Bay, a small seaside village, 40 km from Cape Town, Denis told his mother, Hazel, about me. He told her that he wanted me to come to South Africa and for us to marry. Hazel was a very astute and generous woman. She agreed with him and immediately set out to write a beautiful letter to my mother, assuring her that the family would be thrilled for me to come and that she was certain that they would all love me. Naturally, my family were very concerned. My uncle even phoned me in Ithaca to say that the three women in my life, my mother, my grandmother, and my aunt were in tears. My uncle was also very upset and he upset me too.

I Use the Reparation Money

Hazel's letter was very welcome. Omama, a wise old lady, who had experienced much in her life, made us all feel better. She said, "If it is Anita's destiny to go, then she must go." So, it was that I decided to leave for South Africa at the end of June, when my exams had been completed and to spend a couple of days enroute in Paris with Sonia and Bibi, who were like family to me. I decided to use the reparation money Germany offered to Romanian Jews to finance the trip. At first, I had not wanted to accept the money, but we decided it was for a good cause. My mother was in no position to give me the money for the trip and I wanted to finance it myself.

My promoter, Harry Levin, was initially unhappy at the prospect of my going to South Africa, but eventually, he understood. Furthermore, he had met Denis and had liked him. He arranged that I should do the research for my dissertation on bilingualism and cognitive development in South Africa. Cornell University even gave me a bursary to cover my research expenses. South Africa is a multilingual country and there clearly is great scope for research on bilingualism.

Chapter 10
I Arrive in South Africa

Even though I was emotional and excited at the prospect of meeting up with Denis on arrival in South Africa, I couldn't help but notice the airport ground staff in their brown overalls and berets and lifeless eyes, totally devoid of eye contact when one addressed them. That Denis anticipated this reaction was evident by a short note that he wrote welcoming me to South Africa and which he naïvely asked the pilot to read as my plane approached Johannesburg. This was the land of apartheid and I could not but think to myself that Denis, who I knew was committed to a different kind of society, would have a long way to go before it was realized. Change would come he promised me, but slowly and I believed him because I loved him. And I loved him notwithstanding the reservations of the family that loved me and whose darling I was. And notwithstanding the gentle warning of a colleague of Denis that marrying me would not advance Denis' political career. Yet while much of this was true, Denis was also taking a risk in marrying a Jewish girl with a liberal North American university background. In a way, we were both taking a risk. The fact is we were delighted to see each other again after three months and his family in Johannesburg could not have done more to make me feel at home.

He took me to his aunt Daphne's house in Alberton, in Southern Johannesburg. I noticed all around me was the color of rust, the rusty, dry soil of Africa. Aunt Daphne was Hazel's sister. She was a seasoned businesswoman and owner/manager of Alberton Engineering, having been widowed a number of years previously. She had remarried and she and Uncle Franz and her two children, Nora, and Gerald, welcomed me with open arms. The next day, a Sunday, Hazel's brother Desmond came with his family. They made me feel very welcome. I was particularly comforted when Auntie Nancy said that we even look like each other. "A good omen for a happy marriage," she said. She was right; we have been married for 57 years and happily so.

We left Alberton to travel to Durban and visit the University of Natal, where we both had jobs. Denis had spoken to the professor of psychology, Ronald Albino, who had offered me a junior lectureship. Ronald was a thoroughly English gentleman, who regularly inhaled dried snuff. What surprised me was that the senior lecturer in the department took me aside to tell me that she lived with the professor. They were shortly to be married. But it was a shock to me. Cornell was considered to be a liberal university, but a professor would never dare live with a member of staff, unless they were married. This was 1965 and America was still very conservative. I also met lecturers who were openly gay. Again, something not dreamed of yet in North America.

Universities in South Africa would either be in an English or Afrikaans medium. The English universities, and the University of Natal was one who were openly liberal. They abhorred the system of apartheid and from the beginning I was thrust into intense and heated political debate. Although Denis had often spoken of the conflict between Afrikaans and English speakers, because of historical, religious and language reasons, and although he came from an English-speaking home, he had attended dual medium schools, where both Afrikaans and the English language were used as languages of instruction. It amazed me how many Afrikaans friends he had and the fact that he spoke Afrikaans fluently to them.

At the University of Natal, Denis was considered to be a Conservative because he maintained that if you want to persuade Afrikaners, most of whom supported the National Party to change, you have to understand their hopes and concerns. He believed in speaking to all and so understanding their points of view. For this reason, on his return to South Africa, he had met with Prime Minister Verwoerd, with the Minister of Justice BJ Vorster and among business leaders, Dr. Anton Rupert, the founder of the famous Rembrandt Group, and with Harry Oppenheimer of AngloAmerican Corporation and a previous member of the more liberal Progressive Party. Harry Oppenheimer would become a lifelong friend, who regularly supported Denis in his various campaigns and projects.

Unfortunately, people take sides and at the University of Natal, Denis was considered to be the bête noire of the Department of Politics. By contrast, I was very comfortable at the University of Natal. I enjoyed my colleagues and Ronald and his wife Veronica were very good to me. But I digress. In the first two weeks in Durban, we found an apartment to rent. Denis told me that he had saved R2000,00 and I had to choose whether I wanted an engagement ring or furniture. I chose the latter. Finally, we traveled to the Cape to be married and where I would meet Denis' family and close friends.

Chapter 11
Meeting Denis' Family

It took us several days by car to reach Cape Town from Durban. It was a leisurely trip because Denis wanted to show me the Transkei and the Eastern Cape. We stayed over in Umtata and in East London. I recall that at the hotel we stayed in East London, Indian waiters wore colorful fezzes, obviously a remnant of colonial days.

We arrived in Gordon's Bay to be met by Denis' mother Hazel, a friendly, energetic, little woman, who immediately welcomed me and said that she had her own parent's engagement ring, dated January 1908, and that she was giving it to us as our engagement ring. And as the day progressed, more of the family arrived. Terry, Denis' middle brother with his wife Yvette and their little girl, Sharon, who was four years old and was going to be my flower girl and Bradley, six months old. Denis' younger brother Neil, still a bachelor, also arrived and so did Denis' father, Cecil, who I first mistook to be one of the brothers. He was a youthful, handsome man, who loved driving his Mercedes at high speed.

At first, Cecil jokingly expressed alarm when Hazel told him that we wished to be married in two weeks' time. We explained that there were no reasons why we should wait. I wanted to be with Denis and spending a few months living on my own did not make sense. And my family had objected to the idea that I should wait to see whether I liked living in South Africa. And I knew that I wanted to be with Denis.

Our Wedding Day

We set the date for 31 July, just two weeks away and the venue was going to be in a small, but pretty Presbyterian Church in Somerset West, a dormitory town of Cape Town, not far from Gordon's Bay which the Worrall family and Hazel in particular, regularly attended. I agreed to a church wedding as it was Hazel's wish that we be married in the church where she worshipped. She knew the minister well. He was comfortable with the fact that I am Jewish and that he was marrying us. He even granted my wish to have Schubert's Ave Maria sang during the signing ceremony.

The Worrall family completely accepted me. And in fact, they soon welcomed another daughter-in-law who was half Jewish. Neil's wife, Annalee's father had been a Jewish refugee from the Nazis. We had always believed that there is one God and it is up to the individual to worship as he or she wants. We brought up our children to believe in the same way. We celebrated Christmas and Jewish holidays alike.

We broke many rules! I was alone, without my family. Hazel took me to order my wedding dress. Terry drove me to the church in Cecil's Mercedes and Cecil accompanied me down the aisle. After the ceremony, we went back to Gordon's Bay for the reception. Hazel had arranged for a photographer to take many pictures, so that I could send them to Montréal.

At the reception, I was in a daze. So many new people and so welcoming to me. It was an extremely happy occasion, but I wanted to speak to my mother, a no mean feat in 1965! Denis and I waited for several hours for the connection to Montréal. Eventually, we were able to speak to her. All her life, she regretted not being at our wedding and I've always felt guilty not having been with my family at our wedding. However, my mother joined us a year later, after she was widowed. She spent the rest of her life in South Africa, perhaps her happiest years ever, as she married a lovely man Mike (our kids called him Papa Mike) she was to meet in Johannesburg a year or two after she arrived in the country.

The Worrall family was known for the intense and heated debates on diverse matters, but specifically on sport and politics, and in particular around the lunch table on Sundays. Cecil who had grown up in Woodstock, Cape Town, was very sympathetic to the colored people of the Cape and against government policy based on color. The family was English speaking and supporters of the United Party, in opposition to the National Party and the apartheid government. Denis grew up in a United Party home and as a student he took part in student demonstrations against injustices, such as the removal of the colored people from the voter's roll. When the United Party split to form the Progressive Party, Denis joined it as a student leader.

Chapter 12
Durban: Our Home for a While

We spent a very happy 18 months in Durban. We were newly married, we both had interesting jobs and we had made many friends at the university. We were especially close to the speech and drama department, headed by Professor Elizabeth Sneddon. She had established the first speech and drama department at a tertiary institution and was a formidable lady. The Elizabeth Sneddon Theater is named in her honor. The University of Natal was an island of liberalism in a sea of apartheid. Elizabeth Sneddon used to teach Black and Indian student's drama at the weekend, as they were not allowed to attend the 'white' university. The medical school, now the Nelson R Mandela School of Medicine, was part of the university and I enjoyed teaching the medical students, even though they were taught apart from the other students.

Denis took it upon himself to introduce me to the South African political scene. When Dr. Verwoerd came to Durban, we joined a huge crowd in the Durban City Hall. Dr. Verwoerd spoke for four hours, interrupted only by the shrill voice of a little old lady heckling him from the back of the hall. I was to meet that little old lady at many political meetings. I recall that Verwoerd spoke mostly about Rhodesia (now Zimbabwe), the hot topic of the day. Verwoerd was soon to be assassinated, while in parliament. We also went to hear Robert Kennedy, who, accompanied by his wife Ethel, came to South Africa about that time. The meeting was held in a packed hall at the university. He spoke well, but he was nervous about security. On his way out, we heard him ask his security guard, "Where is Ethel?" They were separated by the throngs that wanted to shake their hand.

As RW Johnson writes in his autobiography, *Foreign Native*, the University of Natal had a small campus and a small budget but many great lecturers.[8] The then principal and vice-chancellor of the University of Natal, Professor EG Malherbe, had been Head of National Security during World War II and had been a close ally of General Smuts. He was for a time Director of UNESCO and his book The *Bilingual School, a Study of Bilingualism in South Africa* is a seminal work.[9] He gave me a copy of his book when he heard of my interest in bilingualism. I quote the book in my PhD—dissertation for Cornell University *Bilingualism and Cognitive Development*, which continues to be a source of international academic interest today. Malherbe was an Afrikaner but was strongly opposed to apartheid and the National Party which was opposed to bilingual schools.

Bilingual schools became a political issue. I experienced this later when I visited the Professor of Education at the University of Pretoria. He made no bones about his disagreement with Malherbe, referring in particular to the latter's research methods. I came home to Durban very deflated.

In mid-1966, almost to the year of my arrival in South Africa, my mother recently widowed, moved to South Africa to be with us. We decided that she should live in Cape Town closer to Denis' parents. We anticipated many moves, before we ultimately would settle in Cape Town and we wished her to settle and establish herself as a beauty consultant in that city. The same year, Denis was offered a promotion to senior lecturer in the Department of Political Science at the University of South Africa in Pretoria. He accepted the promotion, which he would take up early in 1967. We therefore decided to have a belated honeymoon by returning to North America, but first traveling to Athens, and Paris in order for Denis to meet Sonia and Bibi, to London and to Montréal for him to meet my family.

Denis was a great hit with my family and especially with Omama, who was preparing to join my mother and me in South Africa. She had obtained her Canadian passport and her visa to South Africa, when at the age of 82, she had a heart attack and passed on. It coincided with the Six Day Israeli War in June 1967 and I shall always remember the date.

Chapter 13
Life in Pretoria

Not unlike other former colonies, South Africa's government reflects its colonial history in that it has three capitals—a legislative capital in Cape Town, a judicial capital in Bloemfontein, and an administrative capital in Pretoria. This reflects a compromise at the time of the Union in 1910. The Union Buildings in Pretoria has continued to be the seat of government since that date and was so in 1967, when Denis was appointed lecturer in the Department of Political Science at the University of South Africa, which required us to move from Durban to Pretoria, now dominated by the apartheid—supporting National Party Afrikaners, a prospect I frankly dreaded. The one consolation was that driving Denis' appointment was Professor Mike Louw, an urbane and sophisticated scholar who, after graduating from the universities of Pretoria and Chicago spent most of his career as a UN political adviser in South America. Aside from being broad-minded and multilingual and the top political scientist in the country, Prof Louw was married to an Argentinian of Czech origin.

We rented an apartment in Sunnyside, a suburb famous for its Jacaranda tree-lined streets. Sunnyside it seems, was a popular suburb especially for young diplomats and journalists many of them becoming our friends. They sought out Denis' views on the changing political situation and, if I may say so, appreciated my multilingual and multicultural background. We met many young diplomats, who became friends and who invited us to their embassies and homes, and our modest apartment became known for its good food and stimulating conversation. Much of it, obviously, about South African politics. One such invitation remains in my mind. We were invited by the Israeli Ambassador to a small dinner at his residence. Also invited as honorary guest was Dr. Hilgard Muller, the South African Foreign Minister, who I previously mentioned had been a Rhodes Scholar in the classics at Oxford. That evening, I admired the antique artefacts in an embassy glass display cabinet and it was Dr. Muller, the Oxford classicist, who quietly impressed us with his knowledge of what they were and where the artefacts came from.

The University of Pretoria Medical School had a fascinating student body. The students were mostly Afrikaans speakers, poets, writers, and painters. Their spiritual Don was Walter Battiss, the eccentric and bohemian professor of art at the University of South Africa, and a celebrated South African painter. In fact, one such student became an acknowledged Afrikaans poet and a very close friend of mine. He was Dr. Phil du Plessis, who loved my Saturday lunches, where he discovered the joys of Mediterranean food.

I can still see him delighting in my niçoise salad and commenting on how red peppers and anchovies 'make a great combination'. Phil was a good and loyal friend of

Walter Battiss. Upon visiting me in hospital, where I was in for minor surgery, Phil brought me a lithograph that Battiss had dedicated to him. It adorns our living room to this day. Phil became a beloved doctor of the Fish Hoek community where he died. That, of course, was years later, and after Denis and I had settled in Cape Town.

Our five years in Pretoria were happy years and we were in no hurry to start a family. We had careers to build and that was a joint venture. Our love for each other was never in doubt. Although our career ambitions were different, we shared hopes and goals. Denis conceived the idea of a South African political science textbook, the first edition of which was published in 1971. He started a Sunday newspaper column, which ran for a record six years. And he was editor of a monthly intellectual review, which we launched and of which I presently will have something to say.

If the move to Pretoria had one negative, it was that notwithstanding excellent references from Professor Albino of the Department of Psychology at the University of Natal and positive credentials from Cornell, the Department of Psychology at UNISA turned down my application for a lectureship. Quite frankly, the interview didn't go well. I felt applicants trained in South Africa were favored by the department.

It will be recalled that I completed the theoretical part of the Cornell doctorate and had to do the research in South Africa. Being a multilingual country, South Africa required both Afrikaans and English for the matriculation examinations, so I decided to study Afrikaans, and within six months with the assistance of a very capable teacher, I wrote and passed the Afrikaans matriculation paper. With a further grant from Cornell, I was able to appoint an Afrikaans-speaking assistant and start the interviews for my doctorate which was awarded to me in May 1972.

Working on My Dissertation

South Africa is a very bilingual country. My proposal which was accepted by my Cornell professors was to study the cognitive effects of bilingualism on children raised from the very beginning in a one-person-one language, Afrikaans, and English home environment. Naturally, there are many different combinations of bilingualism in this country. For the purpose of my research, I kept to Afrikaans/English bilingualism. The topic suited me as I had experienced bilingualism. I started taking lessons in the French language at the age of seven, right after the war and speaking and writing French were the marks of an educated Romanian, and my mother, despite the shortage of money, hired a French teacher for me. By the time I was 10 years old, I was able to read French books. It helped me a great deal when we arrived in Israel and I decided to attend a French school in Jaffa. Transfer to another language was easy, and I quickly learned Spanish in Havana. Of course, with Romanian, French and Spanish being Latin languages, it is not difficult to pick up Italian.

When we arrived in Montréal, my knowledge of French helped me but within six months, I was able to speak and learn in English, although my home language continued to be Romanian. Omama never learned English. She spoke Romanian or German to her friends.

My mother learned English but was never fluent. Although she read copious amounts of English books, she was never comfortable writing in English. However, she was fluent in French and German. German was the language they spoke at home while her father was alive.

In the latter 1950s, Canada embarked in researching ways to encourage French/English bilingualism. A large research project was undertaken by McGill University in Montréal at the time of my enrollment at the university. The person leading the research project was Professor Wally Lambert. Educated at the University of North Carolina, he worked in Paris and married a French woman. He and his wife spoke both French and English to their children. Lambert was adored by his students and he had a great influence on their chosen field of study. As a teacher, he was casual in his manners (he had the American habit of putting his feet over his desk), challenging, and always encouraging of one's ideas. Over the years, he had many brilliant students, who made a significant contribution to bilingualism as a field of study and research. And I became interested in the cognitive effects of bilingualism. When doing my masters, at Cornell University, I studied whether concurrent bilingualism (two languages learned at the same time) was more effective than consecutive bilingualism (one language learned before the introduction of another language).

I was very fortunate that by the time I reached Cornell University, studies in language and language development were just starting and my promoter, Professor Harry Levin, encouraged me to concentrate on this aspect of child psychology. The cognitive development of a child brought up in a bilingual environment has been of interest since the 1930s when a German philosopher named Leopold, married to an English woman, wrote a book on his observations of his two little daughters, brought up from the very beginning in a one parent one language home environment. Although Leopold's were naturalistic observations, he observed how his daughters thrived in such an environment.

South Africa and Pretoria, in particular, lends itself to such research. When I started, the schools I contacted were very happy to suggest pupils they thought were brought up in such one-parent one-language home environments. Similarly, the parents were more than happy to share with me information about their decision to bring up their children in such a way and expressed their interest in my findings. They were mostly Afrikaans speakers married to English speakers. I was able to find 30 bilingual children between the ages of six and eight and matched them to 30 unilingual English children and to 30 unilingual Afrikaans speaking children. My Afrikaans speaking assistant and I played with the children, while submitting them to a battery of tests.

I found that the bilingual children were very proud of their ability to speak both languages. They were very proud to speak 'Mummy's language' and 'Daddy's language'. On the cognitive testing, they overpowered their unilingual counterparts. An important finding was that the bilingual children were more flexible in their approach to language and more aware of their thinking. When we asked, "Can you call a cow by any other name?" the unilingual children responded, "no, a cow is a cow—you can't change its name," whereas the bilingual children were able to separate the name from the object. "You can call a cow any other name, it still is a cow." In other words, bilingual children reach a level of cognitive development sooner than their unilingual peers.

In today's lingo, they were metacognitive—aware of their thinking. Returning to North America, I presented my findings to the Departments of Psychology of McGill, Cornell, and Harvard Universities. It was also published in the prestigious *Journal of Child Development* and more than 3,800 research papers have mentioned this research.[10] The cognitive impact of bilingualism continues to be of interest. For example, a survey of research in Canada on French/English immersion programs suggest "that French immersion students enjoy significant linguistic, academic and cognitive benefits. " Naturally, there are many types of bilingual education. I limited myself to parents speaking their language to their child from the beginning, in a bilingual home environment.

Chapter 14
New Nation

In the more than five years that Denis spent in the United States, he was impressed with the many intellectual publications which were available and which he missed on his return to South Africa. So, it was that we thought of establishing an opinion magazine which would reflect as much as possible of the entire intellectual and cultural spectrum in South Africa. We decided to call it *New Nation*. And amidst great expectations, and the sponsorship of several major South African companies that Denis persuaded to support the project, the first issue appeared in August 1967 and it carried on monthly until Denis was appointed to the Senate in 1974.

I have said several times that the strength of our marriage, aside from mutual love and respect, has been the fact that we have shared so many things—and *New Nation* is an illustration. It was a one-man-one woman operation, with Denis handling the advertising and the editorial content and I the administrative manager responsible for subscriptions, the mailing and distribution of the publication. In the editorial in the first edition, which Denis cleared with me before publication, he wrote:

"It will be a forum of opinion and commentary spanning the entire intellectual spectrum. Its pages will be open to all opinions without prejudice or favor. Everyone connected with the venture would like to see it grow into a highly sophisticated, tasteful, and intellectually stimulating publication, which will not only be a credit to thinking South Africans but will reflect a truly contemporary image of our country to readers abroad."

And it was indeed read locally and overseas. I personally mailed a copy to just about every university library in the United States and in the UK as well and of course in South Africa. The result is that we received requests for copies on subscription from all over the world.

Professor Andrew Duminy of the University of Natal and one of Denis' best friends recently wrote before his passing, "New Nation was a surprising success and ran for nearly eight years. This was almost entirely due to Denis' great enthusiasm, together with his ability to identify topics of interest and solicit articles from a wide range of people. "

This was also the time of intense ideological rivalry between Afrikaners of the North and Afrikaners of the South—the so-called *verkrampte* (opposed changes) and *verligtes* (enlightened) struggle. Professor Wimpie de Klerk, brother of the future President FW de Klerk, coined this division at a conference in 1966. But it quickly spread to include all cultural organizations and their mouthpieces. *New Nation* could not avoid being involved but I'm pleased to say Denis ensured that it played a constructive and creative role. One consequence is that *New Nation* had a wide appeal among thinking South Africans which resulted in Denis and I meeting and becoming friends with people like Richard Maponya, the famous entrepreneur and his wife, the novelist Nadine Gordimer, Professor Richard van der Ross the future Chancellor of the University of the Western Cape, Jonathan Suzman and his wife Christine, John Dugard, a well-known international jurist, Madeleine van Biljon, the extremely well-connected journalist and Adam Small, famous South African poet who just before his death wrote a very moving poem dedicated to his and Denis' relationship which is quoted in Denis' book, *The Independent Factor.*[11]

One of my favorites was the writer and poet Bill de Klerk and his wife Ena, whom we visited frequently on their farm at the foot of Du Toit's Kloof. My memory of Bill and Ena is tinged in blue, because of the massive blue hydrangeas in their garden.

Our apartment became well-known for its lunches and dinners. I catered myself, mainly from cookbooks, and when in Gordon's Bay, from lessons on the beach from a young culinary expert just returned from London and the Cordon Bleu School, Michael Olivier, who was to become a well-known South African chef and restaurateur.

Our guests came from all over the country and overseas. Among them were academics, politicians, diplomats, and business people, who had the chance in *New Nation* to expound their dreams for a new South Africa. In these get-togethers, Afrikaans and English flowed easily. One such frequent visitor was Otto Krause, at the time, editor of the successful but now defunct magazine *NewsCheck*. He was like the others, fluent and voluble in Afrikaans and English and I was fascinated by how he switched from one language to the other in one sentence. Another frequent visitor was the future minister of foreign affairs, Pik Botha and his wife Helena whom I was to meet in a different capacity later in my life.

Chapter 15
I Embark on a New Career

While I was writing up my research and administering *New Nation*, I became interested in the teaching of children with learning disabilities. I had visited a developmental center in Pretoria and was intrigued by the strategies required to teach children, who were not responding to traditional methods, something more was needed. Existing methods were lacking. In fact, in South Africa, as elsewhere, little was known in the late 1960s on how to teach children who, despite having good intelligence, had difficulty reading, writing, doing math, communicating, or socializing. They were different from the emotionally disturbed children and from children who were mentally challenged. And yet, in special schools, they were not considered to be a distinct group.

Clinics in Canada and the USA were beginning to separate these children into different groups. Parents were agitating and organizations were being set up across the United States and Canada. South Africa was not far behind. In Johannesburg, speech and occupational therapists working at Forest Town School for Learning Disabilities were the first to break away and make provision for children with good intelligence, but who were failing at school. One of the first such schools to be established was by Joyce Fein, a speech therapist who had worked at Forest Town School. Joyce traveled to the USA to learn more about teaching these children. Together with parents, she set up Crossroads School, a primary school with a multidisciplinary team to cater for these children. Two other schools were set up. Crossroads School continues to this day.

When I visited Joyce and Crossroads School, she asked me what I was doing and when I responded she asked, "Why don't you come to work with us?" I agreed and commuted to Johannesburg from Pretoria for two years. I enjoyed the work at Crossroads, the diagnostics, counseling and play therapy. Crossroads School was a beacon of light for these children and for their parents. Education departments from different universities started visiting us. There was intense interest in what we were doing.

During one of these visits from Stellenbosch University, we decided to form an association, the South African Association for Learning and Educational Disabilities (SAALED). I was to become president of SAALED later and with a grant from the AngloAmerican Corporation, I was able to visit clinics in the United States and Canada as well.

Signing the marriage register in Somerset West.

Cutting the wedding cake

Denis' younger brother Neil, Denis' mother Hazel, my little
flower girl Sharon, Norah, Denis' cousin, Cecil, Denis' father
who walked me down the aisle

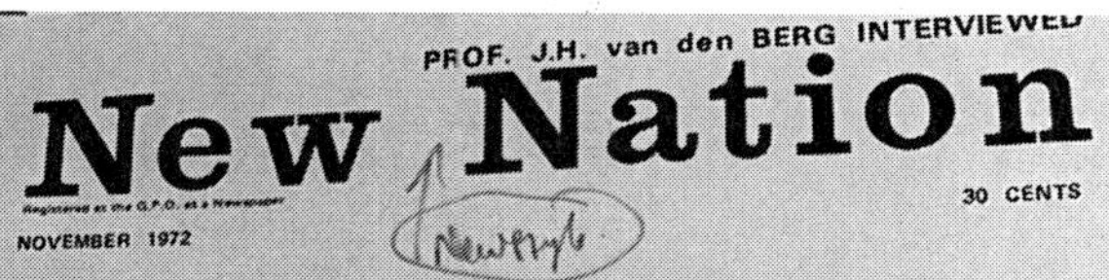

New Nation

NOVEMBER 1972

30 CENTS

SOUTH AFRICAN DIALOGUE REVIEWED

THE U.P.'s NEW POLICY — A PROPOSAL

EDITORIAL

S.A.'s AFRICA POLICY AND THEO GERDENER

The promise of closer relations between South Africa and the rest of the continent, which was in the air in 1971, has now clearly disappeared, and, if anything, there has been a tensing of relations between us. The lack of a sufficiently positive response on our side, the continuance of the SWA issue, the failure of the Rhodesian and British governments to reach a settlement, and China's admission to the UN, all probably contributed to the break-down of the dialogue movement. It may also simply be that the dialogue movement as an alternative to the violence strategy for changing South Africa was premature, and that neither we nor our willing partners to dialogue understood what it entailed.

But whatever the reasons for the break-down, the fact is that short of some major event, like a grant of independence to a Homeland or a change in the status of one or both of the Portuguese territories, no new developments in our Africa relations are foreseeable.

However, without being seen to bend internal policies to meet external factors — something which politicians everywhere don't easily do — there are certain things we can get on with on the reasonable assumption that the present stalemate is temporary.

In the first place we need to formulate both our domestic and our foreign policy goals more clearly, more consistently, more intelligently, and with greater attention to democracy than is the case at present. Dr. Connie Mulder's "New Africa" speech was such an attempt, but much more than this is needed — particularly when patently foolish Ministerial pronouncements on, for example, the right to peaceful protest, clamour for equal attention.

Secondly, the African condition for dialogue (most clearly stated in the Lusaka Manifesto of April, 1969), namely, that before dialogue between African countries and the Republic can take place there should be dialogue within South Africa itself, is a reasonable one; and although the government is right when it replies that there are more meetings today between white, black, and brown leaders than ever before in our history, the situation calls for well-publicised (consultation must be seen to be effective), routine meetings held at regular intervals between the Prime Minister and the official leaders of the other groups. If we are serious about our policy of domestic decolonialism, the time is also long past when South Africans

CONT. OVERLEAF

New Nation, a collaborative effort

We return to Montréal to visit my family

Chris turns one years old.

My mother with her first grandchild, Chris, with Papa Mike.

Celebrating Lyndon's arrival in Grahamstown.

With Chris, Lyndon and baby Dean, in Durban, while Denis was
a candidate for the parliamentary by-election in Durban North.

We are getting ready for another election. This time in Cape Town.

Denis and our three boys. He has just been appointed the South
African Ambassador to Australia.

With the foreign minister Pik Botha, and his wife, at a function
in Pretoria given for us before our departure.

En route to Australia we visit my family in Montréal.

With our hosts, the Taiwanese Minister of Foreign Affairs

Admiring the treasures of the National Palace Museum.

I am presented with a beautiful Chinese vase.

Chapter 16
We Move to Johannesburg and Become Parents

In 1971, Prof Mike Louw was appointed to the Jan Smuts Chair of International Relations which occupied Jan Smuts House on the University of the Witwatersrand campus. It was a very prestigious appointment, with Jan Smuts House housing General Smuts' extensive library. And Mike encouraged Denis to apply for the senior lecturer position in the department, which he did and was successful. He was happy to be back working with real students rather than distance-learning students, as was the case at the University of South Africa (UNISA). And I was relieved that I wouldn't have to commute several days a week from Pretoria to Johannesburg, a trip that used to take me more than two hours. The move was also timely, as we still rented the flat in Pretoria and were looking forward to setting up a home of our own and having children.

Denis' father was a construction engineer and his firm was very active in the Western Cape. In fact, his firm built two houses in Gordon's Bay where he and Hazel had their own house, called Rooftops. He gave one of the houses to

Denis and me and the other to Denis' brother Terry and his family. With a mortgage on the Gordon's Bay property, we were able to buy a house in Linden, Johannesburg. Incidentally, it had at one time been part of a massive fruit farm and we consequently inherited more than 40 fruit trees! It really was an embarrassment of riches but a great place for outdoor lunches.

Denis continued to write a column for the Afrikaans Sunday newspaper *Beeld*, later called *Rapport*. As Denis points out in his autobiography, this column formed a very important part of his career. He was often highly critical of the government—even incurring the wrath of the prime minister. But the editor Schalk Pienaar, whom I also got to know well, courageously stood by him.

I continued working at Crossroads, but after five years of married life, I wanted a baby. And I became pregnant only to lose it when I was six months pregnant. We were both devastated. Denis cried with me when I returned to my bed in the hospital room. We had tried adopting a baby, while we were in Pretoria, but adopting was very difficult. When they looked at our different backgrounds on the application form, they didn't even give us an interview. Nevertheless, we decided that we should adopt, and Denis started using his many connections.

We learned of a beautiful seven-month-old baby boy, who was still in a care home, because he was born with syndactyly (webbed fingers) on his right hand. He had undergone four operations to separate the fingers and the staff who took good care of him, were now looking for a good home for him. We applied—and were successful. We had become the parents of this beautiful little boy, whom we named Christian John after Denis' father Cecil John. My mother and her recently married husband doted on Chris. He was her first grandchild and she was enchanted with him. Her husband Mike, who already had two grandsons, developed an affection for Chris from the beginning.

Our joy was shared by our friends. I was, for example, astonished by the reaction of my friends at work. They were delighted and sent us a huge basket of flowers, bigger than the baby! But I of course was an inexperienced mother. I remember calling a particular friend and telling her, "I've changed his nappy and I have fed him—what do I do with him now?" In those days, there was no or little help for mothers, something I experienced later, when I had Lyndon and could not breastfeed.

We were so delighted to have Chris. His little hand was still in bandages and we had to learn to bath him, while his bandage had to stay dry. A hand specialist reassured me he would not suffer because of his fingers. He said that he could have an operation to straighten his fingers when he was older, if that was his wish.

In the meantime, we had also acquired a lost boxer puppy who in a frenzy, presumably after being hit by a car, came rushing into our garage early one morning. We always wanted a dog, so we took her in and called her Mandy. Chris and Mandy became best friends. His favorite spot for drinking his milk bottle was resting his head on Mandy's tummy as she lay in her basket.

Shortly after settling in Johannesburg, we had to move to Grahamstown where Denis was appointed Director of the Institute of Economic and Social Research at Rhodes University. Incidentally, before Rhodes, he was offered the professorship at the University of Rhodesia, in what was then Salisbury, but I did not see any sense in going to Rhodesia. That country had its own major difficulties. And I had come to South Africa with Denis, who believed South Africa had a future and was committed to working for that future. And as his wife and mother of his children, I was ready to support him achieve those goals.

We Move to Grahamstown and Our Little Family Grows

Before moving to Grahamstown, we took Chris to meet the Worrall family in Gordon's Bay. In those days, we did not fly but traveled by car from Johannesburg to Cape Town. It was a two-day trip with a ten-month-old baby and Mandy the puppy, but the welcome the Worrall family gave us, and in particular, to Chris was worth it. It was decided he should be christened in the little church in Somerset West where we were married. And Sharon, who had been my flower-girl, carried Chris into the church.

On returning to Johannesburg and beginning to make plans for the move to Grahamstown, I discovered I was pregnant and given that I had lost a child, it was very clear that Denis was going to do everything humanly possible to assist me avoid that happening again.

Grahamstown is a university town. But the center of the Supreme Court in that province is also situated in Grahamstown as is the National Monument to the 1820 Settlers. We resisted the temptation to buy an '1820 Settlers' house much like the legendary Guy Butler's, the famous author and English professor but instead bought a large modern house with a swimming pool and modern 'braai' (barbecue) area. It was a beautiful setting and we should have been happy but for one circumstance. While Denis immediately took on several research projects and supervised others, I found myself occupying my days looking after Chris and the house but feeling isolated. I think Grahamstown is like Ithaca, New York; to enjoy it, I would have had to be part of the psychology department, which offered me a lectureship but which I was not able to accept because of my motherly duties.

In January 1974, our second son Lyndon was born in Port Elizabeth, in a lovely hospital run by nuns. Naturally, we were delighted by his arrival. In fact, while I was in labor, someone came to tell me that they had met my husband in the lift. "He was reading a book, but it was upside down!" Hazel and Cecil came to Grahamstown to be with Chris, as our attention focused on Lyndon and they were followed by my mother and Mike, who flew from Johannesburg to see me and our baby in the hospital. My mother was very happy to be part of our life, but also to be independent, with a loving husband at her side. She always said that her stay in South Africa was the happiest period in her life.

I had two children under two years of age which might have been enough for any couple to manage. But just about that time, I began to sense from a lot of little indicators that my husband was beginning to change from being an academic political philosopher to being a politician or at least very interested in practical politics. That is to say that his interest and involvement, while not at the *sturm* and *drang* stage, was more subtle. He definitely was less outspoken. His attitude toward people changed. He was much more tolerant. He sought out particular people to gather their views. As a psychologist, I found this all fascinating but I also found it a little uncomfortable. Life in politics is not easy. Fortunately, Denis was ready to practice law, which he did when we moved to Cape Town.

He continued to edit *New Nation*, which was well-established, and to write his Sunday column for *Rapport*. In 1973, he was named as one of four outstanding young South Africans and I think it was well-deserved: it was for his bridge-building role between Afrikaans and English-speakers. The award was made at a beautiful ceremony in Johannesburg which we both attended, while Chris was taken care of by my mother and Mike. I suppose we are all familiar with the process 'standing for office' which I suppose is mostly obstacle-driven in the United States. While I think it's relatively simple in South Africa—all you have to do is get the support of the party in your district. It wasn't so easy for Denis. He came from a dyed-in-the-wool opposition United Party home and was politically active at university. But he wasn't a member of any political party at that point and hadn't been all those years he was overseas and in the United States. And neither had he joined a party on his return to South Africa. But if election to parliament was a problem, Denis spotted another route.

The constitution provided for the state president to appoint four senators in each province in terms of their knowledge of the indigenous people in the province. And as Denis explained, the challenge to him was to persuade Prime Minister Vorster to nominate him to the president— which notwithstanding the crusty relationship they had over his Sunday column and other matters the prime minister very publicly did! What was pleasing is that we received this news as we visited our good friends, Lola and John Newbury, in East London, with our two babies.

We obviously did not know it then but this step would lead to a dramatic change in our lives—ministerial status, ambassadorships, elections, and eventually, the establishment of a constitutional government.

Chapter 17
We Move to Cape Town but Contest an Election in Durban

The South African parliament is in Cape Town, and as we were about to move with two little children under 25 months of age, I found that I was pregnant again. Thankfully, there was no likelihood of a miscarriage and I was able to live a normal life, even being allowed to drive the car.

We bought a house high up in Oranjezicht, which is the city-facing side of Table Mountain. It looks out to the sea but at the same time has a magnificent view of the city of Cape Town. Dean was born in September 1975, while Denis was occupied in the Senate. Because senators were traditionally elderly, they said Dean was the first baby to be born to a South African senator in 100 years! And as usual, Denis favored the name of an American politician and Dean was named after Dean Acheson, President Truman's celebrated Secretary of State after World War II and somebody my husband admired greatly.

When my third son was born, I felt sorry for myself as it seemed I was destined to be a mother-in-law. As an only daughter, I knew how close mother and daughter can be.

About that time, a by-election was called in the Durban constituency of Durban North and the prime minister asked Denis to stand as the candidate for the governing party. Durban North was an English-speaking constituency and was traditionally held by the opposition United Party. So, it would not be an easy contest but one doesn't turn down a request of this kind from the prime minister. Denis undertook to fight it and to fight a very politically enlightened campaign. And there would be no distractions. The whole family would go to Durban. We rented a two-room suite in one of Durban North's hotels, where the four of us slept in one room, while the baby slept in the other. But I recall many an evening when I returned from a house meeting and Dean had been sleeping, but once he heard my voice, he would wake up and be awake half the night, while I walked with him up and down in the little room. It was tough, but it gave us an idea of what electioneering can be about.

Denis came second in what was a three-cornered race—a credible performance result given that the United Party (UP) had never been defeated in Durban North. In fact, this election signaled the demise of the UP which wasn't going anywhere with the mantra of 'white rule with justice'. This being a by-election, it attracted a lot of media attention which, given my newness to South African politics, I lapped up. What analysts said was that the result signaled a new political order within white South African politics. What they didn't say, was that my husband was going to be one of the top three leaders in South African opposition politics!

Harry Pitman, the Progressive Federal Party (PFP) winner and several of his workers, after the result was known, took off for Cape Town and parliament. I recall praising Denis and his campaign. I wanted him to know that he had done extremely well in a traditionally opposition constituency that had never trusted the ruling party. It was because of his values and arguments that reform could only be achieved from within that party that enabled him to trump the UP and come a healthy second to the PFP, the party of the veteran member of parliament, Helen Suzman. And I encouraged him to immediately fly to Cape Town and to report to the prime minister who, most unusually, saw him on his arrival at parliament and was given a first-hand election report.

Gardens Constituency

Back in Cape Town, while Denis was engaged on a full-time basis in the Senate, he also began practicing as an advocate. On the recommendation of Judge Louis van Winsen, whose registrar Denis had been, he had done his articles with Advocate Gerrit van Schalkwyk. Gerrit and his wife Jocelyn lived a couple of blocks away from us. Like us, they had three little boys, the same ages as ours and we became very close friends. Our boys spent many of their afternoons in van Schalkwyk's swimming pool, where Jocelyn taught them to swim.

Gerrit was Namibian-born and of Afrikaans parentage. Jocelyn was from an English-speaking home and they met while studying at the University of Cape Town. Like many other young professional couples, they detested the government's racial policy and supported the PFP. The political differences between us, and the way we managed them, were to test what was a very strong friendship.

In August 1977, the prime minister called a general election and Denis decided, after an intense discussion with me, to stand as the government candidate in the Gardens Constituency, where we lived. He would be proposed as the National Party's candidate by two very verligte (enlightened) persons, notably Schalk Pienaar, the editor of the Afrikaans Sunday newspaper *Rapport*, and Advocate Dawid de Villiers, who had led the South African team at the International Court of Justice on the Namibian case. He was also the head of the major Afrikaans publishing house Nasionale Pers.

During this time, Chris and Lyndon were attending nursery school together with the van Schalkwyk boys; and since I would be very busy attending to house parties, and chasing after postal votes (there is a very large Jewish care home in the constituency which I elected to canvass), Jocelyn undertook to help me but, given her support for the PFP, she said, "On election day, I will look after your kids, but will lend my car to the PFP to collect their voters." A neat arrangement only friends could agree to. And after the election results were announced and Denis was declared the victor, we went to the van Schalkwyk's to collect our three boys and drank a bottle of wine together. They knew that Denis and I shared the same values with them but unlike many people, instead of simply criticizing the government, Denis had decided to persuade them by joining them.

Also, in 1977, my mother's husband Mike invited us as a family to fly to Montréal and so introduce my boys to the family. Chris had just turned five years old; Lyndon was three and a half and Dean just two. Denis could not take the time off. But together with my mother and Mike, we flew to London and then to Montréal. We returned via Paris in order to introduce the boys to Sonia and Bibi.

Our boys were no angels. My uncle Nelu filmed the boys as they chased each other around Michael's terrace in Saint-Sauveur, in the Laurentian Mountains. We celebrated Dean's second birthday there with the family. My school friend from Israel, Colette was with us. She had joined the Israeli Department of Foreign Affairs and had been appointed consul in Montréal. It was one of those wonderful moments, especially for my mother, who was very happy. The same chasing took place in Paris, but this time, it was around the beautifully set table in Sonia and Bibi's apartment. Fortunately, before breaking any of the beautiful crystal wine glasses, Sonia offered us our coats and suggested that we all go to the park.

My kids were not impressed with London, Montréal nor Paris. They just wanted to chase each other and play. It is as though they knew they would have enough time in the future to enjoy these cities. In the meantime, as Dean was edging toward his third birthday, I decided to go back and start a center like the ones I was involved in in Johannesburg, although more like the McGill Learning Center whose children came to be diagnosed and therapists worked with them.

In 1977, the Israeli government invited Denis and me for an official visit. We met Tidy in Tel Aviv. I had not seen him since I was twelve years old. In the meantime, he had married another émigré from Russia. After introducing him to Denis, Tidy and I walked to a garden for coffee. He asked me how my mother was, and then he said, "You know that I had to wait to marry your mother between husbands." Then he added, "But all is well that ends well." I thought of what my mother had endured to make my life comfortable and I was embarrassed. I think that he could have helped my mother much more.

I suggested that Tidy should visit us in Cape Town to meet our boys. Remember, he was my father. And he followed up with several letters in which he expressed how keen he was to see where we lived and to meet the boys, but that his health did not permit such a long trip. Then for the better part of ten years, I didn't hear from him and assumed that he had passed on, when to my surprise, I was contacted by a South African search company acting on behalf of an Israeli insurance company who, after further checks, advised me that I was the beneficiary of his life policy!

Chapter 18
I Go Back to Work

Madeleine Albright in her memoir, *Madam Secretary,* recalls having often said to young women, "Women's lives come in segments, dictated in part by biology.*"[12]*

Since the move to Grahamstown and followed by Cape Town, I had dedicated all my time to our three little boys. We did not have nannies or au pairs. I was fortunate to have a cleaner, who doubled up as a babysitter when we went out. Besides, I wanted to enjoy our boys' early years and I have never regretted it. In truth, only one of us could follow an occupation, having moved as many times as we did, and this had been Denis. But things were about to change, and I was to implement the benefits of my learning and my exposure to international experts in the field.

The boys were at nursery school until 12 pm and I decided to start a private, multidisciplinary practice for the assessment and therapy for children with learning difficulties. The multidisciplinary practice, with psychologists, occupational therapists, speech therapists and physiotherapists were mostly young mothers, who could only give us so much of their time, provided that the promised time was adhered to. In fact, we provided the opportunity to work flexitime for young professional mothers. And of course, to the benefit of our young patients.

We rented a house, as it happened, it was in Cape Town Gardens, close to our house. We formed an educational trust and I was appointed as director. This was in 1978. As secretary, we appointed a young woman with two young children. Her name was Gabiba Kleinschmidt, and she has worked with me ever since, with a pause of five years, when I went overseas.

In the meantime, to qualify as a counseling psychologist, I had to do an internship for twelve months at the University of the Western Cape; at that time, the university was dedicated to the colored population. Although it was mainly for colored students, most of the professors were white, and so were the counselors.

I recall the first day I went to see the head of the department, himself a school psychologist, to tell him of my plans to open a private educational establishment for assessment and therapy for children with learning disabilities. He interrupted me to say he was not interested in my story.

"One does not establish a private clinic. The Department of Education's facilities is all that we need." (Ten years later, I was surprised to hear the professor's wife asking me whether we would have an opening for her husband, now retired!)

It was true, that the medical council of the day did not allow psychologists, occupational therapists, and speech therapists to form a practice together. I did not understand the rationale behind this. In fact, we went straight ahead, and no one stopped us.

Pro Ed Center was a welcome addition to the Cape Town community. We did not discriminate on racial grounds. Everyone was welcome. Pro Ed Center and later the Pro Ed House School, survived for 42 years. It was closed in March 2021 mainly because of Covid, but also because many schools now have special services attached to them. I am more than gratified to have met mothers, over the years, telling me about their children having attended the Pro Ed Center and now being lawyers, engineers, accountants, or medical doctors. I continued to work at Pro Ed Center until Denis was appointed ambassador to Australia.

The President's Council and Our Departure for Australia

I continued to work mornings and to be at home with the boys in the afternoon. I mostly assessed the children referred to me and counseled their parents. Occasionally, I would be away for conferences but this was difficult as I would have to ask my mother-in-law to stay with them. Quite frankly, although she did this willingly, I would feel guilty and on tenterhooks until I returned home. I recall one time when I was away in Durban and Hazel phoned me to say Dean was in hospital with suspected meningitis. I took the first plane home. Fortunately, he had viral, not bacterial meningitis, and came home with me soon afterwards.

My political duties as a parliamentarian's wife were not onerous, except for the fact that as the wife of a National Party Member of Parliament, I was expected to attend the National Party Women's Club functions. Except for a couple of women, they did not make me feel welcome. I was regarded as different and except for a few, none approached me. I was uncomfortable in their midst as most of the meetings were in Afrikaans, in which I was not fluent. Going to functions together with Denis was also sometimes painful. I recall one situation where a prominent editor walked into the room after having met the men where the wives were sitting against the wall and asked, "All right, who belongs to whom?" I felt humiliated and embarrassed, as any modern woman would have been.

But then, we were part of a welcome development. In 1980, the government, in the face of growing international sanctions, appointed a non-parliamentary commission of inquiry into the constitution with the purpose of creating a more inclusive government. It invited submissions from experts and the general public. Denis was invited to serve on the commission which attracted a lot of attention. It's more important proposal was that the Senate should be abolished and replaced by what was to be called the President's Council, whose members would be elected by the White, Colored, Indian, and Chinese communities. Denis was invited to chair the important constitutional committee. While this was generally regarded as an important step forward toward a constitutional democracy, the omission of Black South Africans was obviously a glaring shortcoming, something Denis was very aware of.

But as he writes in his book "That was the political reality of the time."

The Move to the President's Council

I was delighted with Denis' appointment to the President's Council. We met people from universities who had been appointed commissioners, Professor De Crespigny from the University of Cape Town and his English wife, Rosie, who immediately impressed everyone with her Cordon Bleu recipes. And personalities like Senator Japie Basson, a life-long friend with his wife Clarence, Senator Bill Horak, Professor Richard van der Ross (although we knew him as Dick Ross) from the University of the Western Cape and many more. These were all people committed to ending apartheid and creating a successful multi-racial and multi-cultural country. This was our milieu in which I saw Denis thrive. He was enjoying his work, and his diplomatic skills were honed during this time as he writes in his book "One challenge was that every one of the members of my committee, given the nature of their appointment and previous careers, had large egos, and to manage that I insisted from the beginning that we would work on a consensus-basis".

Given that Denis had ministerial status, and for reasons of security, we were provided with housing on Groote Schuur Estate, a property which Cecil Rhodes gave in perpetuity to the country. The property is large enough to contain several ministerial residences and we moved into a new one we named 'Gardens' after the constituency we had left behind. The boys were enrolled in the South African

College School (SACS), the oldest in the country. But we had barely settled into the house when one day in June 1982 Denis came home to tell me that he had been invited for tea with Foreign Minister Pik Botha who had asked him whether he would consider taking up the ambassadorship to Australia as the incumbent's term was ending and he would need to return to South Africa. I was very surprised and remember responding, "Why would we want to go to Australia?" I was very happy working at the Pro Ed Center and the boys were happy in the new school.

A few months went by when Denis came home to say that the President had personally pressed him to accept the ambassadorship. The President Council's report had been published and that body, Denis was told, would be wound up. The foreign minister also, naturally in confidence, told Denis that if he accepted the Australian position the post as ambassador to the UK, South Africa's most senior diplomatic posting, would be his once it was vacated by the incumbent.

The foreign minister also promised Denis that we as a family would travel to Australia via North America where Denis would spend a month at the SA Mission in New York City and the boys and I would travel to Montréal to spend Christmas there with my family. This was indeed a sweetener, especially as my mother and Mike decided to travel with us. We would all be together.

Presented like this, it was an opportunity we couldn't turn down. But what was interesting was the media reaction to the fact that Denis had been asked to go to Australia with cartoons making fun of the decision. One cartoon showed Denis dressed in colonial garb and Minister Chris Heunis,

the minister in charge of constitutional development and
Denis' boss, with whom he frequently clashed, pointing to
the distance and saying, "Off to the colonies!" Denis denied
it then but now we know that Denis' *verligte* views were
embarrassing to some of the more powerful ministers who
wanted him out of the way, and therefore an appointment to
an embassy.

Chapter 19
Preparations to Leave
for Australia

Moving our household with three children and our boxer Mandy, now 12 years old, was a challenge. We decided that Mandy could not survive quarantine for a year imposed by the Australian government on foreign dogs. Hazel was going to put her on a plane to Johannesburg and my mother and Mike would look after her. In the meantime, as my mother and Mike were coming with us to Montréal, Mandy would go into a kennel.

Another huge responsibility for me personally was the Pro Ed Center. It was running smoothly and was a great success. But with me leaving, I would have to entrust it to someone. One parent offered to look after it together with our secretary/administrator Gabiba.

Denis left for New York soon after we decided to take up the ambassadorship but not before he had asked the Department of Foreign Affairs to allow him to make two trips. One was to visit Windhoek in Namibia, and the other was to visit KwaZulu, the home of Chief Minister Prince Gatsha Buthelezi. Denis insisted that to demonstrate his respect for the Zulu leader, the meeting should be on Buthelezi's home ground. I liked Windhoek and was enchanted by Olga Levinson who, together with her husband, lived in the famous Heinitzburg Castle. A well-known writer and journalist, she told me how much she enjoyed the desert. "Every sand dune has a different sound," she said.

To meet with Buthelezi, we flew to Ulundi, the one-time capital of the Zulu Kingdom where we stayed in what they called the 'Smallest Holiday Inn in the World'. Gatsha Buthelezi is a very urbane man. But back in 1983, he was devastating as a man. For our meeting, he entered the Holiday Inn wearing a cream suit, with brown braided Italian shoes and holding a beaded staff. I was most impressed. We had the opportunity to meet him again many times. On one occasion, when he was the guest speaker at the South African banquet held in the ballroom of the Savoy Hotel in London, I was sitting next to him, he asked me to tug his black-tie jacket if I thought that he was speaking too fast. Incidentally, Gatsha was not the only person to ask me to help at these events. Cabinet Minister Piet Koornhof, who usually spoke for too long, asked me to indicate on a piece of paper how much time he still had—a task easier than tugging Gatsha's black-tie jacket!

Denis flew to the United States ahead of us. I've since learned to appreciate the very taxing job the wife or husband of the diplomat has. The diplomat goes ahead and leaves the spouse to do the menial jobs. Baroness Ewart-Biggs, the wife of British ambassador Christopher Ewart-Biggs, describes this in her memoirs *Pay, Pack and Follow.*[13] And I discovered the truth of it—how the diplomat's spouse has to settle into a new environment, introduce the children to new schools, find appropriate help with the house, identify the best grocer and butcher and appropriate hairdresser, and make new friends. The diplomat takes his office with him, inherits a secretary, and is in constant communication with his home office. Our case illustrates this.

We arrived in Montréal in the dead of winter. Our boys were not used to snow. They thought nothing of going through the snow in their swimming costumes to the inside swimming pool shared by several apartment blocks where we stayed.

The boys were also jet-lagged and would wake up at three am insisting on playing 'Pac Man' on the TV screen. Denis missed all of this but my parents experienced it. When I went briefly to New York City to join him, my mother had to cook bacon and eggs for the children in the middle of the night!

Our sojourn in Montréal ended at the end of January and we left for California (to meet friends in Santa Barbara) and on to Taipei, as we had been invited for an official visit organized by our good friend, the Taiwanese ambassador to South Africa, HK Yang. Then on to our final destination in Australia, the capital, Canberra.

Chapter 20
We Arrive in Australia

After a very enjoyable, personal trip to San Francisco and Santa Barbara, our official visit to Taiwan was most successful. We stayed in Taipei Grand Hotel, built in a Chinese Palace style by Mrs. Chiang Kai-shek. The Vice Minister of Foreign Affairs treated us to a Mongolian barbecue, where the boys were fascinated by the cooking of meat and vegetables in large round solid iron griddle, at high temperatures. The boys were on their best behavior with our hosts. A visit to a three-story building, showing a variety of trade displays was followed by an official ceremony, where I was presented with a beautiful ceramic vase. Chris so charmed our hosts, that they presented him with a similar, but smaller vase.

The highlight of the visit for me was the visit to the National Palace Museum, endowed with the treasures of the palaces throughout China, which Chiang Kai-shek transported to Taiwan. The size of the collection is so vast, that at any one time, only 1% is exhibited. We were graciously escorted by our hosts to Kosiung as well, the largest port in the south of Taiwan, and we were shown through the Shuanghiu Forest area.

After a packed visit of seven days, we left for Canberra. On arriving, we were met by our driver, Mr. Considine, who was going to play a large role in our lives during our tenure in Australia.

The ambassador's residence in Canberra is very elegant. It is built in Cape Dutch style with a huge garden in front of the house and another behind the house. It is so large that it requires two gardeners. The vegetable garden is sufficient to feed the family for the year.

June Kelly in her book *Canberra is a Garden* describes how the Australian states bickered for several years before finally deciding on a site for the capital city in 1909.[14]

In 1913, the site was named Canberra, probably an Anglicized spelling of the Aboriginal word *kamberri*, meaning 'meeting place'. The design for the city was won by American architect, Walter Burley Griffin, after which the man-made lake carries his name.

The story goes that the Australian government decided to build a diplomatic area, close to its parliament, and invited countries to send their designs for their chanceries and the ambassador's residences. South African architects sent the designs which the Australian architects then executed. Our residence and chancery are linked by the garden.

As Denis writes in his book, he could walk in the morning from the residence to the chancery, accompanied by our dogs and armed with his cup of coffee. Our residence is flanked by the American Embassy Residence on the other side of the street, and the Malaysian and Indonesian Embassies on our left, followed by the French Embassy

Residence. I became friends with the Japanese ambassador's wife and I could walk to her residence, when she gave us our lessons in Japanese cooking.

As June Kelly mentions in her book, Canberra has many beautiful gardens, but what I recall most vividly are the flocks of multi-colored parrots flying by our window, the gray and pink galahs in our garden, the laughing kookaburras, and the magpie (although we were always worried about them sweeping on our heads.) And of course, the emu. Once, during a picnic, an emu ate all our sandwiches, brown paper, and all.

But on arriving in Canberra, our first thought was with Mandy and whether she had arrived safely in Johannesburg. We phoned my mother who told us that she had not arrived. In a second telephone call to Granny Hazel, she told us that Mandy had died of a broken heart. The boys and I were inconsolable. We searched for an appropriate tree in the garden under which we could bury Mandy in absentia. The next day, we were on our way to the Royal SPCA to adopt a puppy. The boys decided on a puppy of unknown origin, but so black that we named her Lucy (after Lucifer). One month later, as we went back to the RSPCA for Lucy's vaccinations, Chris called me. "Mummy, Mummy, come and see the Labrador puppies." Of course, we fell in love with one of the puppies and decided to take him as well. Because we were concerned with Daddy's response when we came home with another puppy, and as we were passing by a large mall called Woden with a big sign which read, 'Big W' we decided to call the puppy 'Big W Woden'. We figured that Denis would not resist having a dog called 'big W', and we were right. For the next eighteen months,

Woden would join Lucy in accompanying Denis across the garden to the chancery!

We Settle Down in Canberra

I previously referred to the ambassador's spouse (or any diplomat's spouse for that matter) not having an easy time when he or she arrives in the designated posting. As for me, my arrival in Australia was beset with difficulties in the first three months. First, was the children's schooling. Chris and Lyndon were happily enrolled at St. Edmund's College, a boys' school very similar to what the boys were used to in Cape Town. In fact, Lyndon was in his element and shone in rugby and cricket. However, the school only took boys from grade three onwards, and Dean was only going into grade two. We had to settle for another independent school. Poor Dean, not only was he separated from his older brothers, but also had not yet completed the grade one curriculum according to Australian requirements.

From being one of the first boys in his class in Cape Town, he came home every afternoon shattered because his teacher would say, "You mean, you haven't done this?" or similar put-downs. I was faced with copious tears every night and I decided to go to a government school nearby, Forest School, to talk to them. The principal said, "No worry, we are used to children from different countries, bring him to us." The next day, I took Dean to Forest School and left him. I was anxious all day but, when I went to fetch him, the teacher said that Dean had been happy and he was full of smiles in greeting me. I asked our driver, Mr. Considine, to fetch his books from the other school and we did not look back. If you were to have asked Dean, he would say that the year he spent at Forest School was his happiest year at school.

While I was trying to settle Dean in school, I was obliged to introduce myself to other ambassadors' wives, following Denis' courtesy call to their husbands. Of course, one of the topics of conversation was how the children were settling in and they usually commiserated with me. One of the first items on any ambassador's schedule is to pay an official visit to the Governor General of Australia, Sir Ninian Stephen and his wife, Lady Stephen. We were graciously received.

Back at the residence, I had a chauffeur, two gardeners and a morning char, but no regular staff in the house. The previous ambassador had the use of a couple from Sri Lanka, but once the ambassador returned to South Africa, the Sri Lankan couple was repatriated. It is very difficult to get Australian staff. The residence was a large house, and we needed someone to cook, someone to do the laundry, and someone to look after the boys when we went out.

Social life in Canberra is very full. Just about every night, there are receptions, cocktail parties, or dinners. We had a German caterer, who would come to the residence to cater for big parties and we generally used waiters for cocktail parties at our residence. At one point, the employment agency sent us a Vietnamese, whom we called Mr. T. He was a Vietnamese refugee fleeing communist rule, who had come by boat to Australia, having left his wife and eight children back in Vietnam. We hired Mr. T but he did not like our dogs much and chased Woden with a broom, while saying 'puppy, puppy', causing Woden's lifelong antipathy toward a broom. Every time Woden was shown a broom, he would run away.

Unfortunately, within the space of a few weeks, Mr. T became thinner and thinner, and his coughing warned us that something was amiss. We sent him to be checked and the doctor diagnosed him to have TB and hospitalized him. Our family had to queue up to have BCG vaccinations against TB, something that gave us an immune boost many decades later with the Covid pandemic.

Denis' mother Hazel came to Australia to visit, and she was a great help. Once again, we had no one in the house to help us. Hazel and I were exhausted by the time Mr. T was released from hospital when he announced that the job did not please him. Then one day, the employment agency sent us a young Iranian, called Ali Almasi. He had come to Australia to study and had met a young Australian, whom he had married, and they had a little boy. He was looking for a job and we thought that he was the right man. He and his family became part of our family and when we left Australia, we brought Ali and his family with us to London.

As far as the ambassador is concerned, Denis in his inimitable way, hit the ground running. As television interviews were important, he and the South African Consul General in Sydney, took lessons on how to best appear on TV. TV appearances are an everyday occurrence today, but in 1982, it was something you had to be trained for. Denis' photogenic appearance and his ability to think on his feet made him a television star. He was invited to make speeches on South Africa's future all over Australia. In this way, he cut his teeth in Australia, and it would serve him well in the

UK, as he entered numerous debates with the growing call for international sanctions against South Africa.

With the children, we visited Sydney and had a holiday in Noosa, Queensland. Once Hazel was with us, we took the opportunity to make courtesy calls to the governors of New South Wales, Victoria, Western Australia, South Australia and, on the way to Darwin, in the Northern Territory, we stopped in Uluru National Park to see Ayers Rock. Although the Australian government was not pleased with South Africa and Denis was not devoid of controversy, everywhere in Australia, we were met with courtesy and genuine interest. This was so throughout our stay in Australia. Mary Durack writes in her book, *Kings in Grass Castles*, that during the potato famine, her Irish family had five sons, one emigrated to Australia, one to Canada, one to New Zealand, one to the United States, and one to South Africa.[15] We were treated as family by ordinary Australians.

We Leave for London

No sooner were we happily settled in Canberra than the South African Foreign Minister Pik Botha asked Denis to take up the position of ambassador to the UK. For a long time, the ambassador to the Court of St. James, as ambassador to the UK was called, was the most prestigious South African diplomatic posting. Denis thanked the minister but asked that we should stay in Canberra until the boys finished the school year and he agreed. This suited me too.

By now, Ali was firmly set in our household. He was our cook and general factotum. We were delighted with the

Iranian dishes he prepared and the boys loved him. My mother had come to visit and had enjoyed her stay very much.

My life was in a very satisfactory routine. I had enrolled for a special education diploma at the Canberra College for Advanced Education, now Canberra University, and I thoroughly enjoyed the course. It was led by a wonderful and stimulating man, Max Kemp, a New Zealander, who had studied and worked with Marie Clay, the famous author of the *Reading Recovery Program.*[16] The course was largely on the theoretical and practical assessment and treatment of reading difficulties in children. I would be on the course in the mornings, fetch the boys from school in the afternoons and help them with their homework, and in the evenings, we would attend to the invitations of our diplomatic colleagues and Australian friends.

From the beginning, I attended the Women's International Club of Canberra, a meeting point of Australians and diplomats' wives. I must have made an impression as several months later, I was invited by the Australian president and her committee to be the vice-president of the club. The president is always an Australian and the vice-president the wife of a foreign ambassador. This was a singular honor. The Women's International Club exists in most countries where there is diplomatic representation. It plays a very important function. It is a place where one can meet other diplomats' wives and members of the host country. In Australia, it is traditional that once a year, a country plays host to the Women's International Club itself, and members are invited. The host wants to make an impression on the members and usually brings a fashion show or some entertainment from the host country for the occasion.

I challenged the practice of being ostracized by some members of the club. I asked how it was possible that I, as Vice President of the Club, was not invited to some members' residences. This was true of other countries, for example, Israel. I felt better for confronting them but this practice did not change. It was all very confusing and evidently at the discretion of particular diplomats. For example, the Hungarian Ambassador, whose country did not have diplomatic relations with us, played tennis regularly with Denis. The Turkish Ambassador, another country with which we did not have relations, but whose boys were at the same school as our boys, gave us a goodbye dinner party.

We were very happy and time flew by for us in Australia. As part of our departure, we went to say goodbye to friends in Melbourne, and as I flew back to Canberra on my own, I met Danny on the plane, my first boyfriend, and for many years, the love of my teenage years. I didn't know it then, but he had left Canada and settled with his family in Australia. He was a chemical engineer and was on his way to Canberra, where he was an advisor to the Australian government. We parted ways in Canada, I married a South African and we met in Australia! What a coincidence!

Although we were sad to leave a very happy place, we were determined not to leave with tears. We decided to bring to Australia the wonderful and funny Jamie Uys' film, *The Gods Must Be Crazy*. We hired a cinema and after the film was over, as our guests came out, we served them champagne and petit fours and thus we said our goodbyes laughing. The Turkish Ambassador, whose children enjoyed the film so much in the morning, asked whether he could bring his mother-in-law to the farewell party as well.

We had many farewell dinners and we were sad to leave. We also had to part from Lucy, one of our dogs. We thought that she would not do well in London. She used to chase after buses and cars and she was a risk to bring with us. We advertised and a bus came with a family of six children that adopted her.

We organized a big crate for Woden, and we sent him in advance to London, where he would have to be in quarantine for six months. Before closing the crate, Ali made sure to put one of Lyndon's unwashed rugby socks in the crate, saying Woden should have 'a familiar smell'.

It is a tradition in Canberra to have other diplomats come to say goodbye at the airport. We had about 40 people coming to say goodbye, some of whom did not even have diplomatic relations with our country but were good friends. Enroute to London in August 1984, we visited Manila in the Philippines and Seoul in South Korea, at the invitation of Ambassador Kim and his family, and Tokyo; this latter at the invitation of our wonderful ambassador and a doyen of the Diplomatic Corps, Frikkie Botha, and his wife Monica.

Chapter 21
We Arrive in London

Canberra in July is in winter and getting the family, especially the boys ready for the trip, was no mean feat. We were not dressed appropriately for the more formal wear expected by London. For example, Ali was often in shorts and a shirt, while the children were often barefoot. In the heat of Canberra, electricians and plumbers often arrived wearing just a pair of shorts, no vest, and often barefoot. Furthermore, it was difficult to purchase summer clothes and sandals for the boys, as Canberra was in midst of winter. I promised to buy sandals for Lyndon, who was especially difficult on his shoes, the moment we reached a warmer climate.

We flew to Manila during a humid and warm summer. We all enjoyed riding the jeepneys in Manila, but the traffic was such that we could not get to the hotel soon enough. I recall an old horse next to our jeepney, struggling to breathe and I knew exactly how he felt. The Filipinos are charming people and very friendly. One evening, we were taken to a market and Lyndon chose a pair of sandals. No sooner had he worn them, than they broke and I, being in my Australian mode, suggested to him to go barefoot "We'll get another pair of sandals in Seoul," I said.

As the plane landed at the Incheon International Airport and we prepared to descend, we noticed a band playing. Denis said that this was probably for us and warned us to behave appropriately. We were relieved, however, to hear that the band was to welcome the Prime Minister of Mauritius! However, as we descended the plane, we were asked to go to a certain room, where we were faced with a welcoming group of smartly dressed ladies and gentlemen some attired in military uniforms, who as we entered the room, focused their eyes on our barefoot son and said, "Look no shoes!" Poor Lyndon, a boy of hardly ten years old, was pushed forward and one of the ladies exclaimed, "Tomorrow, we go to buy you shoes." No amount of explaining on how it was that Lyndon arrived without shoes. The next day, we all went to the shopping area, known as Itaewon, and the lady bought Lyndon a smart pair of sneakers. She insisted that we should not offend her by not accepting her gift.

We had a lovely time in Seoul, which was preparing for the 1988 Olympic Games. In fact, we were taken to the Olympic stadium, which was already built in 1984, and were welcomed with a banner "Welcome Ambassador Worrall."

From Seoul we flew to Tokyo and from there we traveled to Kyoto, Hakone, and Nara, where we stayed in a traditional Japanese inn. We were all dressed in kimonos, to the delight of the boys, and we feasted on a Japanese dinner. In 1984, we were not yet used to sushi, shabu or yakitori. It was all new to us, although we had enjoyed tempura at my friend, the Japanese Ambassadress in Canberra.

We landed in London in August 1984 and my preoccupation was once again with the children's schooling. We had tried to get the boys into a school in London but as anyone coming to London in August will know, this is a very difficult thing to do. Someone suggested a school called Hill House in Knightsbridge, famous for Prince Charles having attended there when he was a little boy. The pupils wore knickerbockers, which could only be bought at Harrods, and they played rugby in Hyde Park, still in their school shoes and knickerbockers. Our sons were devastated. Denis and I watched them being welcomed, together with their class in the Pont Street Church, which they used for assembly, and tears were streaming down their faces. They lasted a few weeks, Lyndon having to go with his ten-year-old cohort to Geneva for two weeks. It was all very unfamiliar and he came home very unhappy.

Denis and I went to Dulwich College, where the headmaster had played rugby in South Africa, and where the son of a previous South African Ambassador, Dawie de Villiers (former Springbok captain) had attended. After hearing our problem, the headmaster asked us when we would like to bring the boys. I replied, 'tomorrow', and so it was that our boys were duly admitted to Dulwich College. Lyndon and Dean were very happy but not Chris. He was older and had been placed on age since in the UK, children start schooling earlier than in South Africa. At the end of two years, we agreed when he asked us whether he could start high school in South Africa. Shortly after our arrival, Ali and his family (they had acquired another little baby boy) also arrived in London. Woden was already there, but in quarantine and we would visit him every Saturday afternoon.

Our Official Residence in London— Highveld

The official residence in London of the South African Ambassador (now High Commissioner) was originally built by the Booth family in 1914. They were shipowners, very integrated into London Society, and very musical. Many an evening, the carpet in the drawing room would be lifted to allow guests to dance. Virginia Woolf is said to have often visited the Booths and danced in the drawing room. In fact, the friezes on the ceiling are musical instruments, lyres, horns, and flutes. In a corner, there is a grand piano. It is a beautiful house, rich in history. It was reviewed in the British Architectural Review of 1918 and was described as a 'modern townhouse'.

The story is that General Jan Smuts, who had an eye for good real estate, was informed by his friend, Baron Montague Norman, former governor of the Bank of England, that the New House, as the house was called, was for sale. General Smuts informed the South African government and South Africa bought it in 1946. It was also due to General Smuts that South Africa was able to build its famous embassy on Trafalgar Square. The present stand was occupied by the Morley Hotel, which was for sale. General Smuts, on hearing this, informed the South African government, who bought it. South Africa House, as the embassy is called, is one of the most beautiful embassies in a trophy area of London. Its fiftieth anniversary, celebrated in 1985, was commemorated in a book by Roy McNab, *The History of South Africa House.*[17]

Looking through the filing cabinets, I discovered some notes on our house written by Suzanne Steyn, the wife of the preceding ambassador, Marais Steyn. As I was introduced to many different people who had known Highveld, I met Baroness Norman, who for many years has been a neighbor of the New House. She had written a book called *In the Way of Understanding* and she sent it to me with the inscription, "Mrs. Worrall, who now lives in what I remember as the New House. She told me it felt more like home than an official residence and surely, that is what it was meant to be."[18]

On discovering so many people having such wonderful memories of the house, I asked permission from the South African Department of Foreign Affairs to write the story of the house, and they agreed. The book was completed two years later in 1986. I wrote *Highveld* together with William Lorimer of Christie's who described the house from an architectural point of view and recorded the contents.[19]

Highveld, as the South Africans renamed it, is built on three stories and has 48 rooms and 10 bathrooms. Edwardian in date and Georgian in style, the house is in Camden Hill Road, in Kensington. The basement contains, what in 1984 was considered to be a modern kitchen, and food was transported to the ground floor, which houses the dining room, by means of a dumb waiter, a small lift carrying food and crockery. It is one of the most charming residences in London, with an acre of land, made up of a huge garden and a tennis court. Aside from the beauty of the house and its garden, it contained many beautiful works of art, including several huge paintings by Pierneef, Rowarth, Gwelo Goodman, and watercolors by Kay Butler. To manage this house, aside from Ali and his family, we employed two Filipino ladies, Mila was the cleaner, and Carmen was often the cook.

Unlike in Canberra, we had fewer courtesy calls to make to the other ambassadors, as we have a large expat South African community in the UK. We often gave dinner parties and I was usually in charge of the starters, Carmen in charge of the main course, and Karen, Ali's wife, of the dessert. We discovered that Karen had a real flair for French tarts and the grape tart became one of our favorite desserts to serve at our dinner parties. Ali was the waiter.

Woden eventually completed his six months' quarantine, and together with Dean and Ali, we fetched him from the kennels at Slough. Woden literally jumped for joy to be free and that night he kept us up, while he explored all the 48 rooms. We decided to have him sleep in the laundry, in the basement with the door closed. Nevertheless, during the day he was very much part of the family and we never had a dinner party without Woden being under the table. And no sooner was Woden home, that Ali decided to show him the sights. He delighted to take him walking to Hyde Park. Soon after Woden came home, we were driving on Edgeware Road, when we spotted Ali with Woden. We asked Ali what he was doing there with Woden and he replied, "Mrs. Worrall, Woden needs to know how to travel in the underground." Ali had decided to take Woden with him to have his fitting for a black suit, which we had ordered for him for his more formal attire.

As Denis writes in his book in *The Independent Factor*, "our arrival in London coincided with an intense global anti-apartheid and pro-sanction campaign, which would put as much pressure on the UK and (Prime Minister) Thatcher as it did on South Africa."

Margaret Thatcher was against sanctions but in favor of social and political change in South Africa. She and her Foreign Affairs private secretary, Charles Powell, trusted Denis, and the latter speaking to Charles Moore, Mrs. Thatcher's biographer, refers to Denis 'as the reformist Worrall', and that Denis used to inform them what the South African government planned to do, and in turn, they used Denis to inform the South African government the direction of British policy toward South Africa.

As Denis writes, "Margaret Thatcher thought that reform would only come from South Africa itself and preferred to be seen by South Africa to be a trusted interlocutor, who could help the country move forward. "

Denis adds, "this was the central theme of my ambassadorship in London." I personally met Margaret Thatcher on several locations but I will write more about her later.

But back to the embassy, noisy and angry demonstrators harassed anyone entering South Africa House. This was a daily occurrence with the result that the front door of the embassy was permanently closed and ambassadors and visitors had to go through the back door.

November 2019, thirty-five years later, was the first time we went up the elegant steps of South Africa House, as our present High Commissioner, Nomatemba Tambo, graciously invited Denis to launch his book at South Africa House. You can see large photos of the demonstrators on the walls of the anteroom before entering the grand foyer of the embassy.

Denis was fully occupied going from one crisis to another, while I and the boys settled down to our new life. Martin Skeggs, our driver, who later settled in South Africa with his lovely wife, Henriette, who had been on the staff of South Africa House, was almost fully occupied with driving the boys to and from Kensington to Dulwich and back.

But first, Denis had to present his credentials to Her Majesty the Queen. As she was in Canada, it was suggested to our embassy that he present his credentials to the Counselors of State, who were at that time Prince Charles and Princess Margaret. So, on a rainy day in October 1984, the Palace sent the Marshal of the Diplomatic Corps, Sir John Richards, in a special royal carriage to the embassy, pulled by two beautiful horses. I must say Denis looked very handsome, dressed in a formal suit. I followed in our official car, with a lady assigned by the palace. Our car was supposed to be right behind the royal carriage, when suddenly the heavens opened and torrential rains pelted down on us, and another car came between us and the royal carriage. I learned later that the car belonged to the Head of the Royal Mews, who was concerned that the horses would be frightened by the rain. In this way, we arrived at Buckingham Palace. Denis told us later that the carriage had leaked and he had been concerned about how he looked when he arrived at the palace. But all went well, and after

Denis presented his staff, he and I were invited for a private audience with Prince Charles and Princess Margaret who were very interested in what had been our experiences in Australia. They also asked how the boys were settling in at Dulwich College.

We were to meet Princess Margaret several times later and she always sought us out and was very friendly. In this way, by being introduced first to Prince Charles and Princess Margaret, we were able to get to them know better, than had we just been presented to the Queen. Of course, we had the opportunity to meet Her Majesty several times later and we always found her intelligent and very interested. For example, at the Buckingham Palace reception given every year in December, the Queen, together with members of the royal family, greeted every delegation. We chatted with the Queen, the Duke of Edinburgh, Prince Charles, and Princess Diana. The Queen asked Denis how he had found the horses the day he presented his credentials. She had heard of the torrential rain and the danger that the horses might bolt. Tiaras were in evidence everywhere, but I did not have one. For the occasion, I had ordered a ballgown from the doyenne of the South African dressmakers, Elzbieta Rosenwerth, who sent me a beautiful Thai silk dress, in deep blue. The photographer of the South African *Sunday Times* came to take some photos of us and there is a charming photo of the boys admiring and fixing Denis' white tie before we left the residence.

We Settle in London

All political parties, and most civil societies in the UK, wanted to see reform in South Africa. Denis as a consequence became very popular. His good looks, charming manner and rational arguments made him a favorite on TV news channels and radio. His manner endeared him to many journalists, even some antagonistic to the country.

South Africans, especially business people, were thrilled to have him as their 'Man in London'. Denis had decided early on in his arrival in London that he would work on British business leaders, and virtually every lunch he had was in the City of London. I thought that this applied to all ambassadors, and after meeting some Cameroon diplomats at Buckingham Palace, I naïvely asked them if they were also so busy in the city. They looked at me blankly. In fact, Denis was invited to the city because British business leaders were eager to do business with South Africa. They loved South Africa and wanted it to reform and looked at Denis for answers.

As a family, we quickly settled in London. Lyndon and Dean were very happy at Dulwich College. Lyndon, talented in so many sports, was selected to represent Dulwich in a school cricket competition. Chris, on the other hand, was unhappy at Dulwich. He asked us whether he could start high school in South Africa. We considered it carefully. We had always stayed together as a family and to have Chris in boarding school in Cape Town was a major decision. We agreed, hoping that he would be happier back in South Africa. In January 1986, Chris, and I traveled to Cape Town to enroll him as a boarder at Bishops College, the beautiful independent school in Cape Town, from which I had many clients coming to my center, and consequently, had many friends among the teachers. It was difficult to say farewell to our boy and we were both tearful as we said goodbye, but we sincerely thought that he would be happier at Bishops.

Chris was able to go to Granny Hazel in Gordon's Bay for his weekends. Our friends, the van Schalkwyk's kept an eye on him, but that whole year, with the exception of his coming home for the Easter and June vacations, we were worried about how Chris was doing in Cape Town and where he would be spending the weekends away from school.

Meanwhile, Denis continued to be preoccupied with the threat of sanctions against South Africa. Conditions in the country were not sufficiently improved and Nelson Mandela was still in prison. Denis found the situation depressing. As he writes in his book, he felt let down by his side.

With the Governor General of Australia, Sir Ninian Stephen and
Lady Stephen, when Denis presented credentials as South
African Ambassador to Australia

Making new friends.

The beautiful entrance to the Residence, in Cape Dutch style

With a friend in Canberra.

Denis was often asked to speak on South Africa by the National
Press Club of Australia. They did not always agree with him but
he was so forceful about the fact that South Africa will change
that they took this double photo of him and hung it, along other
of their famous speakers, on the wall coming down
the central stairway.

Hazel Worrall comes to visit us in Australia

Lyndon celebrates his tenth birthday in the gardens of the
Residence with Ali, our chef, babysitter and factotum

Lucy, who used to chase after cars broke her leg. Ali prevented
her from chewing her bandages, with Woden

The Japanese Ambassadress gave me a farewell. With some of
my colleagues from the Women's International Club.

We arrive in London. Denis on the balcony of his Trafalgar Square Embassy.

Denis on the way to present his credentials to
Buckingham Palace

Back at the South African Embassy for a reception

The South African *Sunday Times* sent a photographer to capture
us on our way to the diplomatic corps reception at
Buckingham Palace

With the South African Embassy staff before going to the
reception at Buckingham Palace

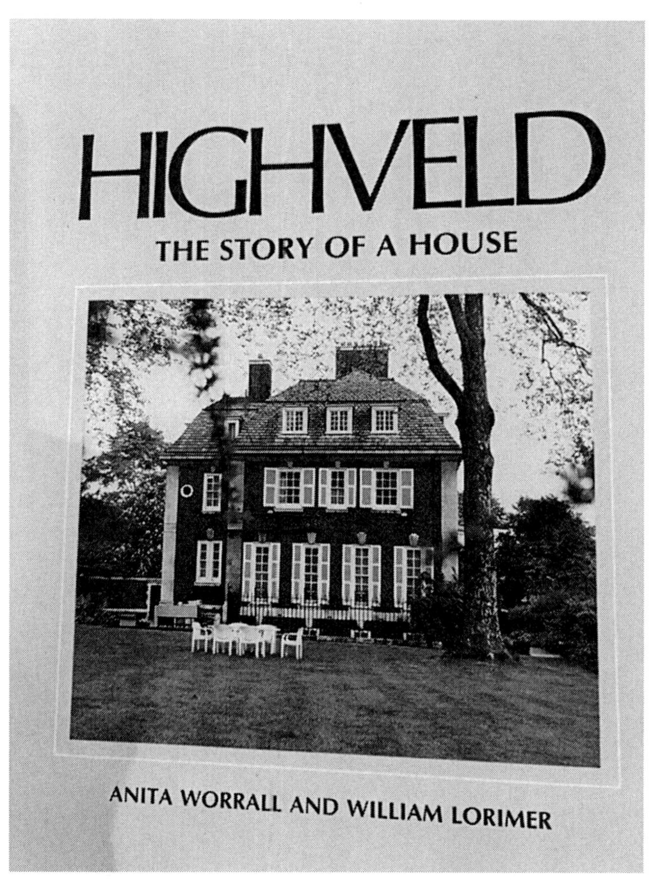

I was especially privileged to write the book on our London
Residence, *Highveld*. I was assisted by
William Lorimer, of Christie's

Denis with Prime Minister, Margaret Thatcher

In front of number No 10 Downing Street

"The time is now" Denis tells the constituents of Somerset West and they responded with great enthusiasm.

Even the skirts carried the name Worrall

The rand went up the day Denis announced his
candidacy in Helderberg

With Gertrude Shope, the President of the ANC Women's
League, in Harare

December 1989 Romanian dictator, Nicolae Ceausescu is toppled. Delighted I write an article for our *Sunday Times* and they took this photo of Denis and I with our boys

In Bucharest with the Archbishop of the Greek Orthodox Church. He received us with visinata and sweet sherbet

A street in Bucharest named after Marcel Iancu. On leaving the country, he changed the name to Marcel Janco as it is easier to pronounce

With our hosts in Bucharest.

PRO ED HOUSE SCHOOL

Pro Ed House School is an exceptional learning environment that focuses on realising a child's full potential.

Our Mission:

At Pro Ed House School we believe in nurturing boys and girls, who learn differently and who are not comfortable in the mainstream, to progress in a safe, encouraging and structured school environment. We do this by recognising their unique learning strengths and by providing alternative and focused learning methods, in an encouraging atmosphere and in a multidisciplinary setting, in close liaison with...

Pro Ed House School

Denis with future President Nelson Mandela, with Wynand
Malan, MP for Randburg

Chapter 22
Getting Acquainted with the United Kingdom: A Startling Beginning

The UK is a compact country and a diplomatic representative may be expected to get to know its major regions and cities, and that is what Denis undertook to do. We decided to start with Glasgow where we had a consular representative but just before we undertook to visit we were invited to attend the Conservative Party's annual conference in Brighton. I was looking forward to seeing Brighton, and especially the famous Brighton Pavilion which I was able to visit while Denis attended the conference.

We were staying at the Metropole Hotel which is next door to the Grand Brighton Hotel where unbeknown to us at the time, Margaret Thatcher and her husband were being accommodated. We had not been invited to the Conservative Party Ball on the evening of 11 October and therefore had a quiet dinner at the hotel, together with our security guard. We were asleep when I heard a loud noise and my thoughts were that it was a bomb aimed at us, planted in the waste bin outside our window. I looked out of the window and saw some women, still in ballroom gowns, as well as men in formal attire, running on the Esplanade. Then, we heard a loud banging on our door and with other guests were asked to leave our rooms and congregate in the basement of the hotel. Denis and I got dressed, took our passports, and were ready to flee. But in the room next to us, our security guard was still fast asleep! We woke him up and proceeded as instructed to the basement, where we stayed for about two hours while security checked that there were no bombs in our hotel.

Little did we know then that the bomb had been planted in the Grand Brighton Hotel, in an attempt to assassinate Prime Minister Thatcher and some of her ministers. As we learned later, the bomb had been hidden on the sixth floor by a member of the IRA, killing five people and wounding dozens. If Mrs. Thatcher had been rattled before, she did not show it that morning! At 9 o'clock and the opening of the Congress, she was poised and ready to deliver a brilliant response to the IRA's attempt at disrupting the UK's ruling party's annual conference.

Travels to Scotland and Northern Ireland

Denis and I often traveled to Glasgow and we got to like the Glaswegians. We always enjoyed going there and visiting our Consul General and his wife. They always held dinners for us to meet interesting people, for example, the Queen's Painter and Limner, a position in the Royal Household unique to Scotland, David Donaldson, and his wife Marissa. They loved South Africa and David often exhibited here. We became good friends.

I particularly enjoyed the Burrell Collection, a museum in Glasgow. It houses the eclectic collection of Sir William Burrell and his wife, wealthy Glasgow shipping magnates, who chose 360 acres of parkland to house the collection. It is a beautiful museum, where the glazed windows, and the park beyond, fuse to share the beauty of the collection.

On one occasion, we were introduced to several people, who on learning that I was Romanian-born, insisted that we meet with King Michael of Romania, who had been king of Romania on two occasions. Once as a little boy, when his father, King Carol II was exiled to Paris in 1930 because of his liaison with Mrs. Magda Lupescu. However, King Carol returned to Romania in 1936 and reigned until 1940, when he abdicated, and Michael, once again, became king. In 1947, as he disagreed with the communist control of the government, he was asked to abdicate. He left Romania, with his mother Queen Elena, a cousin of the Duke of Edinburgh, to attend Queen Elizabeth's wedding in 1948. He settled in Switzerland, and he was linked to the Moral Rearmament Movement. He was invited to Cape Town by our friend Japie Basson, who invited us to lunch at the parliament with the king and his wife, Queen Anne. The king was very impressed that I spoke Romanian to him.

Our new Glaswegian friends suggested that we invite King Michael and his wife to Highveld when he visited London. And we had an occasion to do so when King Michael and his very friendly, Queen Anne, came to visit us at the official residence. We chatted for a long time, and he expressed the hope, which was soon to be realized, to visit Romania once again. I shared that hope and said that I would want to visit the country of my birth again.

Our visit to Northern Ireland took a different turn. Denis decided that we should go as a family and that we should drive through Northern Ireland, and on our way, visit his mother's relatives in County Armagh. We had driven without any thought of security, when suddenly, just before County Armagh, we were surprised by several Royal Constabularies on motorcycles. They insisted on accompanying us for the rest of the trip. This is how we arrived in Belfast, and to our home for the duration of our stay, which was the royal residence, Hillsborough Castle. We were presented to our chef and our butler, and as neither the Queen nor the Duke were in residence, Denis and I were assigned to the Duke's bedroom, separated from the Queen's by a bathroom. The children chose three different bedrooms. Security was very strict. I had to ask security for permission to visit the famous gardens, where the Queen Mother had delighted in planting peonies and the royal children had planted trees. They said, "Of course, but you need to be accompanied," and so I was escorted to the royal gardens by a guard with a rifle.

Celebrating Shakespeare's Birthday

The birth of William Shakespeare, the great English writer, has been celebrated in Stratford-upon-Avon since 23 April 1816. Ambassadors and High Commissioners to London are invited for a two-day celebration in Stratford. It is a beautiful and colorful ceremony, with the streets decorated with the flags of many nations, South Africa being one of them.

Our culture minister at South Africa House, who previously attended the celebrations in lieu of the ambassador, suggested to Denis that we should attend as a family. On 21 April 1985, we drove with the boys, but without our driver or a security guard, to attend the celebrations. However, on arrival at our hotel, we were met by several detectives and policemen, who were to stay with us, as they anticipated demonstrations against South Africa. They told us that during the street procession and the unfurling of flags on 23 April, we would be separated and that a detective would accompany Denis to unfurl the South African flag, while the boys and I would be accompanied by another detective on another street. They also informed us that armed policemen would be stationed on the roofs of buildings along the streets, where the flags of nations were to be unfurled.

The celebration consisted of a lunch, attended by Princess Margaret, who recognized Denis and me and was very friendly. The actor, Ben Kingsley, fresh from acting as Gandhi, in the movie of the same name, was the guest speaker. I recall he made a snide remark about South Africa!

That night we all attended the play *As You Like It* and the following day was the anticipated procession to the Holy Trinity Church, where Shakespeare is buried. On 23 April, the streets were colorfully decorated with the flags of many nations. The boys and I were separated from Denis, and with a detective, we followed the mayor, who accompanied Ben Kingsley. The latter was assigned to unfurl the flag of Ethiopia. We followed the mayoral group but all four of us were concerned with what was happening to Denis. The boys kept on asking me whether Dad was okay and I assured them that he was accompanied by a detective and that there were policemen on buildings to spot any troublemakers.

At the stroke of midday, the flags were unfurled by the representatives of the nation they represented. As we were behind the mayor, we were amused as Ben Kingsley attempted several times to unfurl the flag, only for it to come falling down.

Eventually, we were reunited with Denis, who told us that as his detective was a distinguished and well-dressed man, he was taken to be the ambassador, and the heckling and insults were directed at him. In the afternoon, the procession continued to the Holy Trinity Church, where Shakespeare is buried. Much relieved, we joined Denis for the first procession to the church, once again avoiding the hecklers. Seeing us embarrassed, the ambassador of the Netherlands, and his wife, surrounded us to prevent the hecklers from getting to us. It was a beautiful and memorable experience and we were grateful for the care of the detectives and the police and for the kindness of the people who accompanied us in the procession. The culture minister concluded that the South African Ambassador will henceforth not attend these events, of course, that was before the transformation of South Africa into a fully democratic state.

Social Life in London

When we arrived in London, it was the embassy's tradition for the ambassador's wife to be the president of the

South African Women's Club. I took the position very seriously and met with our embassy wives very often.

Wives of the Diplomatic Corps met at the 'Welcome to London International Club'. The story was that after World War II, General Eisenhower suggested the formation of such a club as part of international cooperation, and the club's motto is 'understanding through friendship'.

Kathleen Evans, the wife of Leo Evans, the number two at the South African Embassy, was extremely helpful. Having arrived some time before us, she not only assisted me in entertaining the wives of the embassy staff but also introduced me to her friends.

I enjoyed meeting and working with women from all over the world. It was a lesson I learned from my experience in Canberra. Soon after my arrival, I decided to host a lunch at Highveld, for several presidents of other international clubs. We all enjoyed the lunch and we asked, "Why don't we do this more often?" This was the beginning of the Federation of International Women's Associations of London (FIWAL). It was founded in 1986 and it acts as an umbrella organization of women's associations in London and the surrounds. The purpose is to have combined events. I co-chaired the first combined event, held in June 1987. FIWAL is now a much-respected association with thirty international clubs affiliated with it. I flew over to London to attend the 25th anniversary.

An important reason I enjoyed London was because of the variety of people there. At one dinner party, we laughed when the hostess, an Iranian, said that we were all misfits. That was true! Here I was a Romanian, married to the South African Ambassador, in London! The misfits made the most wonderful hostesses, such as the beautiful Lady Nina Martin, a Venetian, who had married an Englishman, whose drawing-room was a veritable eighteenth-century 'salon' where ambassadors and other embassy personnel, as well as locals, met regularly.

As the wife of the ambassador, the hostess often sits next to the guest of honor. They would often tell me what they did not have the opportunity to tell the ambassador. It was on one such occasion when we were invited to lunch by a neighbor of Harold McMillan, former prime minister, and the author of the *Winds of Change* speech to the South African parliament in 1960. In the famous speech, he told the South African government that his government would not stand in the way of independence of Her Majesty's colonies in Africa and that it did not support the South African approach to race relations.

He was in his nineties, when we saw him, and was preparing to make a speech to the House of Lords. He made several allusions to the speech at lunch. After lunch, as was customary, the ladies withdrew to powder their noses and the men remained behind to chat and drink port. After about half an hour, the hostess said to me, "Anita, you must also meet Uncle Harold." She brought him to the drawing room and we sat together. He told me how much he had enjoyed his visit to Cape Town on the Union Castle ship and asked what the name of the hotel was, associated with the Union Castle, and I said it was the Mount Nelson Hotel, famous for its beautiful gardens. He paused to think and, after some time, he told me, "You know that fellow, your prime minister (meaning our President Botha), he is right. He is reforming, but it takes 100 years before you get it right.

Your country is on the right track." On the way back to London, Denis was driving the car and I asked him what Uncle Harold had said, after the ladies had left the room. Denis replied not much. I told him what Harold McMillan had said to me. He stopped the car, pulled over, and asked me to repeat the story!

We enjoyed several dinners with Harry and Bridget Oppenheimer, chairman of Anglo American and a great philanthropist at their beautiful flat in Eaton Square. One such dinner, to which we were invited, was given in honor of the Prime Minister, Mrs. Margaret Thatcher, and her husband. As we stopped to admire the painting of a horse by George Stubbs, Mrs. Thatcher admired my two-piece dress. I told her that it was from Cape Town, made by Elzbieta Rosenwerth.

There were many beautiful moments we experienced in London. I recall being awakened at seven o'clock every morning by the sound of the House Cavalry riding by, as they exercised the horses. I loved the traditions. I experienced one such tradition in Woodstock, the village where Blenheim Palace is situated. It is the birthplace of Winston Churchill and the seat of the Duke of Marlborough. We went for lunch at a coaching inn, called The Bear. It is one of the oldest in England, dating from the thirteenth century. After a superb lunch, I went upstairs to refresh myself and I noticed the charm of the place but that the wooden floors were creaking. I returned downstairs and I happened to bump into the manager, and I commented that the building was so charming but perhaps it was time to attend to the creaking floors. "Oh no," replied the manager.

"We only attend to the wooden floors every 200 years and they were attended to last century."

We bought a tandem bicycle to ride around London. It was great fun. Denis did the pedaling and I sat on the back saddle, thinking that should he want to get rid of me, this was the moment, what with all the buses and taxis speeding by!

We rode past South Africa House and watched the demonstrators shout outside the buildings. They didn't recognize us. We also rode past the Savoy Hotel nearby and we were shooed away by the porter. Little did he know that he was shooing away an ambassador! On the way home, we would stop at the French bakery to buy croissants for the boys.

Family Holidays and Denis Increasingly Frustrated

We had family holidays in south-west France, Collioure, and the following year in Skiathos, Greece. Both were full of concerns for Denis. Denis was called back to London from Collioure to announce the South African President's intention that he was about to make significant changes to South Africa's government. It was expected as the foreign minister put it that he was about to 'Cross the Rubicon'. We cut our holiday short so that Denis could prepare the media for the announcement.

In the end, for some reason only the President knew, the speech was changed and it was a huge disappointment. I remember Denis trying to justify the change, as was his duty as ambassador, and I sitting at the BBC with Helen Suzman saying, "How can he say these things with a straight face?" knowing full well that he did not believe his words.

The following year, we traveled to Skiathos in Greece. Throughout our two-week stay, Denis was pensive. He was reading the biography of Jan Smuts, a former prime minister of South Africa, a close confidant of Winston Churchill during WW II, and whose statue is close to Churchill's in front of Westminster Abbey.

I knew that he was toying with an idea. He was deeply disappointed in the news from home and was increasingly frustrated.

In the latter 1980s, there was a great deal of ministerial activity between London and South Africa. South African ministers came and went, and they were often accompanied by their wives.

It is customary for embassy staff to prepare an itinerary for the minister, but not for the wives. Sometimes, if I thought that the wife would enjoy meeting some of my contacts, I would organize a lunch, as I did for Antoinette du Plessis, wife of the Minister of Finance, Barend du Plessis. Often, I would be left to my personal busy schedule. Some of the wives I genuinely enjoyed. One who springs to mind is Lulu Koornof, wife of Piet Koornof, then Minister of Co-operation and Development. She asked me to accompany her to Oxford University to collect the PhD diploma of her son, who had been a Rhodes Scholar. It was a lovely trip and on the way she showed me where she had lived in the early years of her marriage with her husband, Piet, who had also been a Rhodes Scholar. We were invited to tea at Rhodes House, a beautiful house designed by Herbert Baker, also the architect of South Africa House in

London, and modeled on a Cape Dutch farmhouse. This was a memorable visit and clearly very important to Lulu Koornof. She was so excited in anticipation of receiving her son's diploma that she tripped and fell on the stairs going to the university registrar's office. Fortunately, she was not badly hurt.

Former President FW de Klerk at the time, Minister of Education in South Africa, and leader of the Transvaal National Party, came to London with his first wife, Marike. Denis asked the number two at the embassy, Leo Evans, and his wife to meet them at Heathrow. In the course of the morning, Kathleen Evans phoned me to say that Mrs. de Klerk had been very offended by us not having prepared an itinerary for her. I was not accustomed to preparing an itinerary for minister's wives but I quickly made a plan to accompany her to the Wallace Collection, one of my favorites. As our official car was busy collecting the boys from school in Dulwich, I took a taxi to the museum. In the taxi, she broke down and confessed that, "I'm not like you, Anita. I can't get in a taxi on my own." I commiserated with her, but I became aware of how spoiled our ministers and their wives were, being nearly 50 years in government.

I recall the wife of the minister of defense helping herself to the ambassador's phone to call South Africa, without so much as asking me. That phone, sitting on his desk was only intended for the personal use of the ambassador to connect to South Africa.

Chapter 23
The Eminent Persons
Group (EPG)

It was very clear that, given her attitude toward South Africa, Margaret Thatcher would be alone in opposing all-out sanctions against South Africa at the Commonwealth Heads of Government meeting in Nassau in May 1986; and by way of a compromise, it was decided to send an 'Eminent Persons Group' drawn from the Commonwealth countries, whose task it would be to kickstart talks between the South African government and representatives of the black community in South Africa. A major goal would be to ensure the release of Nelson Mandela. Denis writes "the importance of the EPG was understood by everyone at the Embassy in London, but less so by the South African government."

The mood was jovial at a lunch given in London by the Secretary-General of the Commonwealth, Sir Sonny Ramphal, for members of the delegation just before their departure to South Africa, to which Denis along with Carl von Hirschberg from the Department of Foreign Affairs in Pretoria were invited. I too was included, and as I mentioned before, was embraced by General Obasanjo former President of Nigeria, who congratulated me on my South African husband's athletic achievements in representing Nigeria in the one-mile competition in the annual Nigerian/Ghana universities athletic competition!

As I said, the mood was jovial and optimistic. It was clear they were all looking forward to going to South Africa and expecting to make a contribution to the South African problem as they saw it, and specifically bring about the involvement of Nelson Mandela. Denis accompanied the mission to South Africa the next day and began participating with it in discussions with prominent government and opposition people—but insisting on a meeting with imprisoned Nelson Mandela. President PW Botha was not going to agree to this and decided to sabotage the mission by ordering the SA Airforce to bomb ANC camps in Zimbabwe, Zambia, and Gaborone. His message was clear and the next day, the meeting between the EPG and the SA government was a total disaster and Denis ended the visit. He flew back to London on a flight that included some members of the EPG.

I recall that I met Denis at the top of the stairs at Highveld and said to him, "You have been sabotaged!" He tried to explain what had happened, but I could see on his face how disappointed and dispirited he was. It was against this background that one afternoon shortly afterwards, Gavin Relly, the chairman of Anglo American and a person whom we had got to know well, visited us at Highveld. He proposed that Denis take over the directorship of the South African Foundation, an organization supported by South African and international business. It was a very tempting offer. However, I agreed with Denis that he had a different role to play in South Africa. He had not yet given up on reform. He knew that the South African voting public was more ready for change than the government gave it credit for. Gavin repeated his offer in November 1986 over drinks at Hotel George V in Paris, while we were on our way to the opening of the Delville Wood South African WW I Memorial in Longueval, France.

Also, about that time, the foreign minister phoned Denis to ask whether he would take up the post of ambassador in Washington. Denis took the call in our bedroom as we were preparing to go out to a dinner. The foreign minister explained that, given his performance in Canberra and London, Washington now required his skills. Without looking at me, Denis responded in Afrikaans that his mood for politics was low and Washington was a big change. We had to consider our boys and their schooling.

What I did not know at the time was that Denis had made up his mind. His career as a diplomat had been successful. No doubt he would have enjoyed Washington very much. But now he wanted to return to South Africa and to politics. He was waiting for the opportunity.

Denis Resigns

Denis returned to South Africa several times, but in December, we all went home on leave to Gordon's Bay. In our little flat there, Denis took me aside to tell me of his decision to resign and to stand as an independent in the upcoming national elections in May 1987. He knew that the South African electorate was ready for change and he was going to approach every constituency to support him in his stand.

I knew that Denis was unhappy with the pace of reform and the manner in which the government was treating its friends, but I was not expecting this. I told him that the National Party 'would run over you like a bus.' He told me that he had spoken to Anton Rupert, the founder of Rembrandt Tobacco, and to Harry Oppenheimer. Through the years, he had a close relationship with both. They were willing to help, but Anton Rupert, echoed my sentiments saying, "*Die Burger* is going to kill you." He also told me that Jannie Momberg, a former chairman of the SA Cricket Association and sponsor of Zola Budd, the former barefoot runner for Britain at the Olympic Games in 1984, had phoned him to encourage him to fight for the seat of Helderberg and that he, formerly of the National Party, would be his manager. Helderberg Constituency, arguably the most beautiful in the country, included Gordon's Bay and Somerset West, the seat of the Worrall family. Between us, we would be assured of 12 votes! But there were other constituencies to be had. Helderberg was the constituency of Minister Chris Heunis, the second most powerful man in the government, and he was popular in his constituency. Taking this challenge reminded me of an American friend, who when visiting us in Durban, said that, "Denis is like the salmon, always swimming against the current." I felt that he had made up his mind.

We returned to London and Denis made preparations to resign. The Court Circular released from Buckingham Palace on 31 January announced his resignation and this was a bombshell. Journalists in the UK, South Africa, and internationally went wild. Some were fearful for Denis. Gerald Shaw of the *Cape Times* wrote, "Denis Worrall plans for high stakes." The same Court Circular announced the death of Harold Macmillan, the former prime minister, and my companion at a lunch a few years before. We attended his memorial at Westminster Abbey and many ambassadors wished Denis well. The Japanese ambassador's wish was memorable. Approaching us, he bowed low and said, "To new life, Ambassador."

Buckingham Palace sent signed framed photos of the Queen and of Prince Philip. The Marshal of the Diplomatic Corps made the point that this gift was only for ambassadors who had completed five years in London. Her Majesty had made an exception as Denis had only served a little over three years.

We decided to tell the boys before they had heard from their friends or from the radio. Dean, who was in the middle of his junior exams, mentioned that he had wished that I had not told him on the morning of his exam. But I thought that hearing from me was preferable to hearing from someone else. The news of Denis' resignation was all over. Although the boys took this in their stride, ten-year-old Dean, told his father, "Dad, I hope you know what you are doing."

When the news broke, the phone at Highveld did not stop ringing. Denis was receiving congratulations from all over the world. Friends from Cornell University, whom we had not seen for years phoned us. We decided that I would stay until the boys completed their term. I was reminded of Baroness Ewart-Biggs and her book *Pay, Pack and Follow*.

Denis said goodbye to our friends at a black-tie dinner at Highveld. The mezzo-soprano, Elizabeth Howard, also a friend, offered to perform on the occasion. An offer we gratefully accepted. Denis left London on 13 February 1987. He remembers that as the plane took off, he wept as he hadn't for ages. Stanley Uys, a South African journalist in London wrote, "Denis was given a rough ride during his ambassadorship, but even his opponents conceded that in style and content, his ambassadorial performance was in a class of its own."

Denis started his campaign in the Helderberg running. Somerset West was abuzz with offers of constituents to work for his campaign. My sister-in-law, Annalee Worrall, brought all her friends to work at the campaign office—and she had many friends!

But just as we were about to leave London, I received a call from somebody at the Conservative Party headquarters in Smith's Square, asking me whether he and a few other members of parliament could visit us.

Shortly afterwards, four Conservative Party MPs came to tell me that Mrs. Thatcher had appreciated the work Denis had done during his ambassadorship and wanted to do something for him. She proposed sending her most senior party organizer in Scotland, who was about to retire, to help Denis.

I phoned Denis to tell him of the visit and Mrs. Thatcher's offer. I knew that Denis would be hesitant because he knew he would immediately be accused by the ruling National Party of bringing foreigners into a South African election and this would be used against him. I suggested to Denis to say that Sir Graham wanted to write a book on the South African election and in this way, no one would know what his actual mission was. One of our election sponsors, Dr. Robert Hall, invited Sir Graham to stay with him and his wife on their beautiful farm and also arranged a car for him.

His electoral acumen was clearly evident and he participated in many less obvious ways.

The election staff—especially the ladies—loved the charming silver-haired old Scott.

At the end of March, the boys, Woden and I departed for Cape Town. We said goodbye to our wonderful staff. Ali and his family returned to Australia. Martin Skeggs married his South African girlfriend in the embassy and moved to South Africa, where we see them often and count them among our closest friends. Woden, unlike his move to the UK from Australia, did not have to stay in quarantine. He traveled with us and when we landed, the boys and I went to the back of the plane to re-join a delighted Woden.

Chapter 24
Federation of International Women's Associations of London (FIWAL)

There are many international women's clubs and associations in London. That was the background against which I invited seven heads of these international associations to lunch at Highveld. We had a great time and we asked ourselves, why don't we do this more often? And this is how the FIWAL was born. It has its goal 'to broaden friendship, understanding, and communication among international women's associations in London'. FIWAL has recently celebrated its 35th birthday. It is in effect an umbrella association of 30 international clubs with a yearly combined event committee in which all the clubs in London could participate.

I became co-chair of the Combined Events Committee. That year FIWAL decided that the combined event would be a seminar held at the Institute of Education, University of London. The theme was *Women Today. What have we gained? What have we lost?* Through the Pakistani women's club, we approached the venerable Chinese-born

Eurasian, Madame Han Suyin, to participate as well as the politician and author Baroness Ewart-Biggs and Dr. Bryan Lask of Great Ormand Street Hospital, a child neuropsychiatrist, and the driving force behind designing a battery of neuropsychological assessments for eating disorders. The seminar was planned to take place on 10 June 1987. Of course, Denis' resignation made it very difficult for me. However, Gavin Relly at Denis' request made sure that my return flights to London, prior to the seminar and on the day of the seminar, would be subsidized by Anglo American Corporation. We had three meetings of the combined events committee and I attended all three. I would spend one night in London, only to return to Somerset West to work on the election the next evening.

The interest in London in the Helderberg election was enormous. Each time I returned, a passport officer would ask me, "How is the election going, ma'am?" Our friends in London supported us. In the course of the election, I received the following letter from the President of FIWAL; "You are so much in the thoughts of all of us. We never meet without enquiring if anyone has the latest news of the South African election. Every news bulletin is reported and TV coverage is discussed. How I wish that I could just buzz down and help."

On my return to Somerset West, I threw myself into the election campaign. I accompanied Denis to house meetings where my presence was important because women were the majority of Denis' supporters. They were concerned about the future of their children. The result was we created a group called 'Women for Worrall' and had a big rally. Unbeknown to us, Lord William Rees-Mogg, former editor of *The Times* and at that time columnist for *The Independent*, attended one of our meetings. He was so impressed by the quality of the women attending that he wrote a very favorable column on the election. In the *Sunday Star* of 9 August 1987, Magda de Wet contributed an article in which she called me 'The Ace Up Denis' Sleeve!'

Our boys did not have such a comfortable time! As soon as we arrived, Lyndon and Dean joined Chris at Bishops. They stayed with us in Gordon's Bay but had to commute 53 kilometers on the back of a bakkie of one of our supporters. On the night of the election, they slept in front of the fire at the home of one of our friends. The election results came out at 3 am. Denis lost by 39 votes out of 18,000 and there was no recount. Denis and his advisors felt that he had achieved what he set out to do; South Africans were ready for a major change!

I involved myself in opposition politics. Aside from fast-emerging political leaders of color, I found myself at home with politicians like the veteran liberal politicians, Colin Eglin, Helen Suzman, Frederick van Zyl Slabbert, Tiaan van der Merwe, Dave Gant, Dene Smuts, Zach de Beer, Tony Leon, and many more.

I Travel to China and to Harare

The first FIWAL Combined Event took place on 10 June 1987, and I flew to London to participate. It happened to coincide with the Conservative Party's third election win and Mrs. Thatcher was delighted. Sir Graham invited me to the Conservative Party headquarters in Smiths Square to experience the celebrations. Obviously, it was a very jovial and happy occasion for them, with champagne and orange juice flowing freely. A clearly very pleased, Mrs. Thatcher arrived to a tumultuous welcome. She thanked everyone and then, pointing to the newly carpeted floor, she said. "Now is the time to celebrate…but mind not to spell any juice on the carpet!" The Iron Lady showed her feminine side!

As Denis' performance showed, he had support across the country and with the help of individuals like Jannie Momberg and his wife Trinie, Enid Le Sueur, Koos Myburgh, Jenny Newton-King, Annalee Worrall, Dave and Gill Gant, several wealthy farmers, business people and many more, Denis established the Independent Party, which very soon had the Progressive Federal Party looking for a merger, which happened with the creation of the Democratic Party, the forerunner of the present main opposition, the Democratic Alliance.

In October 1987, members of the Welcome to London International Club were invited to visit China by the wife of the Chinese Ambassador to the UK, following a very successful trip to China by Queen Elizabeth and Prince Philip the previous year. I wanted to go with the group, but South Africa had no diplomatic relations with China. The Chinese travel agent, who was organizing the tour, did not give me much hope, but in September, she phoned me in Cape Town to say, "Okay, you come." I was delighted and flew over to London and from there to China with the group. I was hesitant on arriving in Beijing, as the passport control officer was not happy with my South African passport (I had long given up my Canadian passport, as I felt that I should hold the same passport as my family.) Through the intervention of the Chinese travel agent, I was allowed to join the rest of the 40 odd members of the group.

I was one of the first South Africans to enter China. Colin Eglin, leader of the PFP, preceded me. Our group visited Beijing, Shanghai, Xian, Guangzhou, and Guilin. At every stop, I tried to phone Cape Town, but we clearly had no communication between the two countries. Ever hopeful, when I arrived in Guangzhou, I asked the hotel operator to connect me to South Africa and she assured me that she could connect and shortly phoned back saying, "Your call to South Korea, Madame." I gave up and I asked a friend's husband in London to phone Denis and explain the situation.

In 1987, China was still very under-developed. There were millions of bicycles and not a car in sight. In Shanghai, I was nearly run over by a bicycle when I stopped to cross at a light. In Xian, the only hotel available to stay in was a Stalinist hotel, with a huge dining room, more like a canteen. For money, we had to exchange our cash for 'Friendship Money' which could only be spent in 'Friendship Shops' and in these shops, it was very difficult to gain the attention of sales ladies who showed no interest in us. Yet around the hotel, we noticed intensive business activity, in an all-night market, and we realized what this would mean for China and the world once the Chinese spirit would be allowed to range freely. The country would boom, as has happened. As I visited China several times, subsequently, I actually saw this happening.

Back in Cape Town, we bought a beautiful house in Rondebosch. The boys joined Chris at Bishops College and

Chris became a day boy like his brothers. I became involved in the politics of the Democratic Party and when the Institute of a Democratic South Africa, IDASA, started by Alex Boraine and Frederick van Zyl Slabbert, two former PFP Members of Parliament, invited me to join a group of 53 South African women 'to meet ANC women in exile' in Harare, I jumped at the chance.

On arrival at the hotel and having been assigned to our rooms, we were asked to come down to register. With some others, I took the lift, which opened at a different floor and five lovely women entered saying, "Hi, we are from the ANC." My shock was real. I was accustomed to reading in the media about 'atrocities' committed by the ANC, and although I was here to meet them, I was still surprised to see them welcoming us. Of course, I got over the initial shock and for the next three days, we made friends.

I met people I had not heard of before but were to become household names. People like the leader of the ANC women in exile, Gertrude Shope, Frene Ginwala, soon to become the first Speaker of the House of Assembly of fully democratic South Africa, Barbara Masekela soon to be appointed Ambassador to France by Nelson Mandela, and many more.

As it happened, the partner of Wimpie de Klerk, brother of President FW de Klerk, was also in our group. We waited together for our luggage in Johannesburg, which took a long time to arrive. Eventually, the luggage arrived, but that evening, wanting to show Denis the ANC literature I had collected, I realized that my suitcase had been searched and the literature removed! The following day, the Minister of Police took a swipe at us during his speech in parliament, calling us 'useful idiots'. In other words, the implication was we were naive and credulous 'do-gooders' who could be manipulated for the ANC political agenda. Ironically, a term that was first used by Lenin.

Denis was elected as one of the three leaders of the official opposition Democratic Party and we had ringside seats in Pretoria at Nelson Mandela's inauguration on 10 May 1994 as president of a fully democratic South Africa.

While Mandela was still in prison, he telephoned Denis and me to thank us for the Christmas card we had sent him. When Denis asked him what he should call him, he said, "Call me Madiba."

Chapter 25
I Go Back to Romania

On 25 December 1989, Romanian communist dictator, Nicolae Ceausescu was executed and Romania was freed from the shackles of communism. It has since joined the European Union and took its place, once again, among the Western European states.

Naturally, I was delighted when Ceausescu fell and I was prompted to express my feelings in an article that the South African *Sunday Times* accepted and published on the front page under the heading, 'My Country is Free Again'. Accompanying the article was a beautiful photograph of Denis and me and the three boys in our house in Gordon's Bay.

The South African Department of Foreign Affairs almost immediately established diplomatic relations with Romania, appointing as ambassador, Peter Cilliers, who had served with Denis in London and whose wife, Marlyn was a friend of mine. Soon, the Foreign Minister, Pik Botha, requested me to make an official visit to Romania. Of course, Denis as one of the three leaders of the Democratic Party opposition, and the leading spokesman of the DP for foreign affairs, was to accompany me.

We arrived in Bucharest in September 1991. We were greeted with a red carpet from the plane to the arrivals building, and Marlyn Cilliers, having boarded the plane immediately it landed, handed me a bouquet of red roses. What a contrast to the experience I had as a tearful twelve-year-old, when I left Romania with my mother and grandmother, from the dark, unlit cattle train station, on our way to an unknown future!

We traveled in a convoy of cars, Denis, with the ambassador in the first car, and Marlyn and I followed in another car. Good hotels were scarce in Bucharest at that time and we were taken to a hotel for the 'nomenklatura' i.e., reserved for high-status officials.

Nonetheless, this was our experience the next morning when, speaking in Romanian, I called room service to ask for breakfast. But only one breakfast arrived. I phoned again and asked if it was possible to have another breakfast, as we were two in the suite. The waitress, who took my call, arrived with another breakfast, but I heard her shouting the length of the hallway, "They want two breakfasts! They want two breakfasts! So much work, so much work!" Food was also scarce. We were served the same stew for lunch and for supper.

Yet, I was treated like a celebrity. I did radio interviews, we were taken to the Romanian parliament, were received by the Greek Orthodox Archbishop of Romania and, in his palace, nuns served us with traditional dulceata, a fruit sweetness, which took me back to when I was a little girl, visiting my aunts. We were received by the Prime Minister, Petre Roman, the first prime minister since 1945, who was not a communist, and by the foreign minister, at the time Adrian Nastase. The meeting with him was broadcast.

We were driven to Brasov and to Poiana Brasov, already an international ski resort. At Poiana Brasov, we were served bear meat, which I gently declined, as I recalled, when I was a little girl and I saw bears made by their handlers to dance in the street, begging for money.

One can't visit Romania without seeing traces of Ceausescu's rule. He was a terrible man. He had one-fifth of Bucharest destroyed, including schools and churches, to build the so-called House of the People. He was executed before the project was finished. The 'grand avenue' leading to the House of the People was deliberately made wider and longer than Champs Elysees in Paris. At the time, we visited the shops on the avenue. They were not well stocked, but we did buy some beautiful Romanian carpets.

The palace was huge. One of the halls was as large as a football field. Ceausescu envisaged himself walking toward his guests, he entering the room from one door and the guest from the opposite door! An army of artisans was entrusted with the woodwork. Next door to that huge building was the Palace of Science, in honor of Ceausescu's wife Elena. She had aspirations of being a scientist!

For many years, the government wasn't sure what to do with the building. When we were there, the rumor was that Robert Maxwell, the newspaper baron, wanted to buy it for his empire. Recently, the Romanian government decided to transform it into the Palace of Parliament.

I asked Marlyn to accompany me to find the various places I recalled as a child. When I asked my aunt Dida what was the name of the street that they had lived in Bucharest, she could not remember. She had suppressed that whole period in Bucharest, from the war to the communists! She said that it was too painful to recall.

I surprised myself at how well I could recall places where I and my relatives had lived. We went to visit my grandparent's house, where my mother had first met her father when he returned from the camp where he was interned as an enemy alien. I saw the school I attended as a first grader, Notre Dame de Zion, now used for some ministry.

I asked the driver to take me to the apartment house we had moved in after my parents' divorce. It was all boarded up. The following day, I asked Denis to come with me to see it. He looked at the boarded apartment house and delicately said, "Well, you have come up in the world, my darling!"

It is amazing how much I remembered! I saw myself, a little girl, walking with my grandmother to visit my uncle Nelu and his family. I found the house that my aunt Dida found too painful to recall.

Possibly, the worst part of Ceausescu's commitment to grand ideas which I knew from my studies of children, was his ambition to grow the population of Romania manyfold. He thought that a large nation would naturally be prosperous. So, he and his wife decreed that no woman could have an abortion unless she was over forty years old. The security police would ensure that younger girls did not have abortions. This resulted in women trying to abort themselves with the accompanying damage to the fetus. Some women used large knitting needles to abort and the babies were born with damaged limbs or heads. Hunger and damaged babies resulted in the notorious 'orphanages' where abandoned babies and small children were dumped.

I asked to visit an orphanage in Bucharest and was taken to one which was in a mansion in Bucharest, which I suspect was one of the best orphanages. Despite this, I saw children rocking, not being able to hold their heads up or emotionally flat, with no expression on their faces. Some children could not talk. I shall always remember a boy of about twelve in a wheelchair, his head leaning on his chest, as he could not hold it up, addressing me with the traditional respect 'Sarut mana, Duamna'. (I kiss your hand, Madam). It was heart-rending.

We left Bucharest with a heavy heart. Somehow, our hosts did not know that I am Jewish. On another visit to Bucharest, many years later, I asked my driver to take me to Templul Choral, the big synagogue in Bucharest, where my parents were married.

This time, on reaching Budapest for a short visit, we asked our ambassador to arrange a visit to the ghetto, in the center of the city, and the beautiful Dohany Street Synagogue, in the process of being restored, with the adjacent tree with silver leaves engraved with the names of those murdered by Nazis.

That night, in a Czardash restaurant, when the band played My Yiddish Momme, I became so emotional that I wept.

Chapter 26
I Return to Pro Ed Center and Start a New School

While I was in Australia and the UK, the Pro Ed Center had continued. It was appreciated by the Cape Town school community but without committed leadership, it had started to flounder and the board invited me to return to being the director. With my former assistant and friend, Gabiba Kleinsmidt, we returned to run Pro Ed Center.

The general view is that findings from scientific research in education take at least twenty years before being put into practice. I had always believed that education is the way to transform people's lives; and South Africa was and is in desperate need for more good schools and good teachers.

Due to my theoretical and research background in the field of education, I strongly believed in incorporating new findings into practice, as soon as possible. Furthermore, I have always admired good and sensitive teachers, especially in the early primary school years, when teachers literally change children's brains by teaching them reading, writing and maths. We have neurological evidence of this fact.

As an educational psychologist, when I arrived in Canberra, I enrolled in a special education diploma course offered by the Canberra College for Advanced Education (now the University of Canberra). It was a one-year course and the director was a New Zealander, Max Kemp. In his reading lab, I was assigned to teach a ten-year-old boy who had reading difficulties. I was not allowed to assess him with the battery of tests generally used by educational psychologists. I simply had to teach him to read! I enjoyed the task but I don't know how much help I was to him.

In the 1980s, the method of teaching reading was the whole language approach, which de-emphasized the teaching of phonics. I tried to make the experience pleasant by allowing him to select his own books, according to his interest. I even asked him to dictate to me a story which I typed out and asked him to read back to me. Because the story was dictated, it was easier to read by guessing the dictated words to me. Writing for reading is a good way to encourage a reluctant reader to read, because he does not have to decode new words. Unfortunately, my student needed a good, structured literacy program, which was not available at the time.

Max Kemp in turn had been a student of Marie Clay, the Auckland University teacher, who devised the *Reading Recovery Program* used for early intervention with 'at risk' children. The program was acclaimed in New Zealand and Australia and in the late 1980s the British government, sensitive to the low reading scores of British children, invited her to set up her program in Britain, and I was privileged to meet her at the Institute of Education in London. She told me that it was a successful program for most children, but that at least 5% of the children did not benefit from it. She was an elderly lady by the time I met her and she exclaimed, "If I had another few years, I would crack that one too." Although she did not label the children in the 5%, we know now that she was referring to those children who have dyslexia, a neurobiological condition.

The study of dyslexia was advanced in the 1990s with the findings of Professors Sally Shaywitz[20] at Yale University in the USA and Maggie Snowling[21] in the UK. This was transformative research and changed our perspective of reading failure. Dyslexia is a deficit in language processing, and to overcome it requires specialized techniques. Furthermore, they were able to show authorities that dyslexia and intelligence are not linked. Bright children can be dyslexic. These findings coincided with my return to Pro Ed Center.

I recall one mother, with five-year-old identical twin boys. They required both occupational therapy, as well as speech therapy.

The mother would sit for hours in our reception room, waiting for the boys to finish their lessons. We joked saying that she had become one of us.

One can imagine my pleasure when, many years later, I received a message from the mother to say that her sons had successfully graduated from the University of New South Wales.

The identical twins gave us a lesson of the reasons for a child's resilience and motivation.

Although identical, one twin was able to mainstream from grade one, while the other had to be schooled in a special-needs school for a few years. He joined us when we became a school and was successfully mainstreamed three years later. We tried to figure out why one twin was able to be mainstreamed from the very beginning of his school career, while his twin could not. They had the same genetic make-up, the same intrauterine environment, as well as the same very supportive parents, yet one had the confidence to mainstream, while the other had not. I believe that confidence was instilled by the teacher in the one who was mainstreamed early. Being twins, they were in the same school but in different classes, with different teachers. I always thought that teachers have an enormous role to play in encouraging the child to develop the 'growth mindset' i.e., 'To err is good'. 'You learn from your mistakes'. This encouragement gives the child the ability to look forward and to try again.

We Open Pro Ed House School

Although in the 1990s, the buzzword was 'inclusivity', i.e., schools should be able to teach all children, regardless of the difficulties they had, we knew that although, in theory, inclusivity is desirable, it does not work as the teachers are simply not trained to teach children who learn differently.

I attended many conferences of the British Dyslexia Association, where Professor Maggie Snowling and her co-workers presented their seminal work, which showed that the lack of phonological awareness and lack of understanding of the sound structure of the language is the cause of most reading disorders. Pro Ed House School was the first in Cape Town, and arguably in South Africa, to use speech therapists to teach structured literacy.

About that time, I was elected National President of the *South African Association of Learning and Educational Disabilities* (SAALED) and I invited Professor Snowling to South Africa to address the National Conference. I wanted my South African colleagues to hear her, to share with them her and her colleagues' significant research.

In 1998, I decided to open a full-time specialist unit, an independent primary school, for bright children who had difficulty learning in the mainstream school. Initially, our school was accommodated in two houses, which had been converted into a warehouse. Denis encouraged me to buy those buildings by creating the Worrall Family Trust. Eventually, we bought the adjacent property to the warehouse. It took time to make the warehouse child friendly and I thank my colleagues for their contribution in that regard. Our aim was to support the children until they were ready to try again in the mainstream school. I did not believe in opening a high school as I believed that children, with appropriate support, could return to mainstream once they were able to believe in themselves and to learn. Of course, that implied that they came to us in the early grades.

We opened the school with one learner and one teacher. At the end of that year, we had 17 children in the school and we were growing. The children were mostly dyslexic, with attention deficit hyperactivity disorder (ADHD) and autistic. Today, we describe them to be *neuro diverse*. We had one principal and four teachers. We did not have a student in grade five and when the mother of the future South African Olympic gold medalist phoned me to ask whether we could enroll her son in grade five, I told her that I did not have a grade five yet. "Well," she replied, "you have one now." He spent two years with us, was successfully mainstreamed and after earning several degrees, was part of a group of South African rowers, who earned a gold medal at the 2012 Olympics in London. His mother telephoned me to tell me the news and I asked her whether he would speak to our children and their parents. Our assembly hall was full when her son spoke about how Pro Ed House School had helped him to realize his potential.

It had given him the confidence and the skills to learn despite his challenges. The children admired and wanted to touch his gold medal and their mothers were in tears.

This has been the refrain of many of our learners. The years spent at Pro Ed House School had made it possible for them to feel good about themselves, to taste success, and to go on learning. Our classes were small, the teachers and therapists shared a common language of classroom practice through weekly in-service training.

With its first government, the ANC government decided that teachers who wished to receive retrenchment packages could leave the profession. This was the early ANC government's biggest mistake. Many experienced teachers took the package, retired, or started independent schools. Pro Ed House School was fortunate to inherit some of these teachers, they were well trained and devoted teachers, who contributed a great deal to the development of Pro Ed House School and its students.

Although many of our students were dyslexic, there were also some who had been diagnosed with ADHD or with both conditions. I became interested in ADHD when I was at McGill University, one of the first Departments of Psychology in the world to study this condition. One of my lecturers, Virginia Douglas in a paper based on her research and read at the Canadian Psychological Association in 1971, argued that deficits in sustained attention and impulse control were more significant of the disorder than hyperactivity. Prior to that, it had been described as Hyperkinetic Disorder. Thanks to the findings of Virginia Douglas, *the Diagnostic Manual of the American Psychiatric Association* (third edition) took the position that hyperactivity was no longer essential for a diagnosis of ADHD, i.e., it can occur without hyperactivity.

The treatment of choice has been Ritalin (Methylphenidate), a stimulant. Although a schedule six drug, we know that it is not addictive and for the children who need it, is a blessing. They can concentrate, while the medication is in their system. Because of my experience with ADHD, doctors would refer to me to assess, diagnose and to recommend the medication. Because the literature on Ritalin has been controversial and the Church of Scientology spent huge amounts of money to protest against the use of stimulants to children, including Ritalin, often parents were hesitant to use Ritalin for their children. I developed a Ritalin/ Placebo trial, over ten school days, with daily observations by the teacher and the parent. Neither the teacher, nor the parent, knew whether it was a Ritalin day or a Placebo day, and I was able to show that, for many children, diagnosed with ADHD on the days that the child was on Ritalin, teacher and parents ratings had improved. The parents were reassured by the results of trials.

Naturally, medication is not the only treatment. Structure and routine at home and at school is as important. I also trained parents and teachers on how to manage their children with ADHD.

I was invited to present the results of the trials at the International Conference on ADHD, held in Jerusalem in 1995. At the conference, I met many of the international authorities on ADHD, such as Professor Russell Barkley, the author of many books, and the undisputed expert on ADHD.

The Ritalin/Placebo trial had come to be used by many doctors in South Africa.

Altogether the school was a success. We taught our children that the brain learns from mistakes. One of our grade three children, challenged by a maths problem, exclaimed out loud, "I made a mistake! My brain is growing!" We encouraged children to adopt the 'growth mindset', that intelligence and skills are not fixed and that they are improved by 'effort'. We taught them how it feels when you put in 'effort'. We supported them to understand the way they learned and we taught them how to plan, monitor and evaluate their work. Most significantly, we taught them strategies to learn.

Chapter 27
A Thinking School:
Transforming Education in
South Africa

It is important to recognize that what we offered at Pro Ed was largely based on the international connections my colleagues and I built over the years, starting with Donald Hebb, Virginia Douglas, and Wally Lambert at McGill University, with Harry Levin at Cornell University, and with Max Kemp at Canberra University. Others included, Reuven Feurstein in Jerusalem, Maryanne Wolf, Russell Barkley, Carl Hayward, Kathy Greenberg, David Heyerle, in the US, and with James Anderson in Australia and with Maggie Snowling and Bob Burden in the UK.

In the late 1980s, I joined a few academics, among them the Professor of Physics, Willy Rautenbach of Stellenbosch University, and the Professor of Education at the University of Witwatersrand, Mervyn Skuy, who were all gravely concerned at the state of education in South Africa and were convinced that all children require a cognitive approach to teaching and learning. I became a member of the *International Association for Cognitive Education Southern*

Africa (IACESA) established in 1988, shortly after the establishment of the *International Association for Cognitive Education* (IACE) in Canada and the USA.

IACE was influenced by the teaching of Professor Reuven Feuerstein, in Jerusalem, who, having worked with children who had survived the horrors of the Holocaust, advanced the belief that all children can learn.[22] He developed the theory of *Structural Cognitive Modifiability*, in terms of which he maintained that structures of the brain can be modified as a result of deliberate intervention from a skilled mediator, a parent, a teacher or a member of the community. In fact, Feuerstein predicted what we know today as neuro-plasticity. He had proposed a program called *Instrumental Enrichment* to stimulate thinking skills in children. In the United States academics such as Professor Carl Haywood, of Vanderbilt University developed *Bright Start*, a cognitive program for children from four to six years designed to equip them with cognitive skills for learning.[23] In turn, Professor Katherine Greenberg, of the University of Tennessee developed '*Cognet*', a series of mini lessons to introduce cognitive skills to classes.[24]

IACESA conferences brought them, as well as many other authorities in cognitive education, to South Africa, and many of us attended conferences in Israel, United States, Finland, and Belgium.

In 2004, Gill Hubble, Principal of St. Cuthberts College, in Auckland, New Zealand, encouraged whole school training in cognitive programs. She selected two programs, David Heyerle's, '*Thinking Maps*'[25] and Costa and Kallick's '*Habits of Mind*'[26]. '*Thinking Maps*' are a set of systematic visual tools that correspond to eight cognitive processes, such as brainstorming, sequencing, classifying, cause and effect, part-whole relationships and seeing analogies.

'Habits of Mind' are a set of 16 attitudes and dispositions that successful people have mastered, such as finding humor, flexibility, managing impulsivity, thinking interdependently (together), remaining open to continuous learning and so on. This approach adopted by St. Cuthberts was successful and persuaded other educators that whole school training was the answer to encourage cognitive education in schools.

In 2011, I was president of IACESA, and we were busy organizing the national conference to take place in July, when Emeritus Professor Bob Burden, of the University of Exeter in the UK, came to tell us that several educators in the UK, along with the University of Exeter, had decided to develop *'Thinking Schools'*, where the whole school embraces the cognitive approach. Following Burden's visit, several of us attended conferences in the UK and visited schools that had adopted the *Thinking School* curriculum.

I invited David Hyerle, Professor Bob Burden, and Art Costa to the IACESA National Conference, held in July 2011 in Cape Town. Art Costa could not come, and he suggested that we invite Australian James Anderson, a director of Habits of Mind Institute which is in New York. The conference was the largest national conference ever organized by IACESA and, amid much excitement, a proposal was accepted that *Thinking Schools South Africa* (TSSA) should be established. TSSA is a non-profit organization with a director whose job is to train South

African schools to become Thinking Schools and I was nominated chair of the National Board of TSSA.

In 2011, TSSA's goal was '100 Thinking Schools, which would develop 200 000 thinking children'. In the last ten years, we exceeded the numbers. However, the Thinking School concept is adopted by and large by independent schools, and Pro Ed House was such a school. It is the teachers in the government schools that we think should have whole school training. We need to influence the various education departments in the different provinces.

But, as I said at the start of this chapter, research in education takes many years to filter through to those who are in charge of the curriculum in education departments. In the meantime, South Africa is in desperately needs to introduce cognitive education to its disadvantaged learners. There are wonderful exceptions. My co-founder in TSSA and colleague, Dr. Louis Benjamin, is hard at work training teachers to stimulate preschoolers in remote and disadvantaged schools.

In 2019, Pro Ed House School was awarded The Global Thinking School Status, from the University of Exeter in the UK.

We asked whether other special needs' schools had been awarded this status. They responded that Pro Ed House School was the first to receive this award.

In looking back over my life, I left a secure and comfortable existence with my family in Montréal to join Denis in a faraway, and very troubled land. My family having accepted my decision, did not oppose it but assured me that, should I not be happy I would be welcomed home.

Immigration and risk-taking is engraved in Jewish genes. My mother showed enormous courage in leaving her family, once to escape communism and the second time to join her only daughter in remote South Africa. Amazingly, my grandmother, Omama Marie, was prepared to join us in South Africa, when shortly she passed on.

As for me joining Denis in South Africa, it was an enormous step for a girl who was steeped in the liberal tradition of universities in the North East of Canada and the USA. I loved him and I believed in him and his promises. He kept his word that things in South Africa would change and he played a not so small role in this change. Unique in the world, the South African electorate showed its resilience by handing power to the majority.

The End

References

[1] Hughes, Maureen (2010) *The Countess and the Mob, The Untold Story of Marajen Stevick Chinigo and Mafia Lord Rosselli,* iUniverse United States.

[2] Sandqvist, Tom, (2006) *Dada East—The Romanians of Cabaret Voltaire,* MIT Press USA.

[3] Sebastian, Mihail (2012) *Journal 1935–1944 The Fascist Years*, published in association with United States Holocaust Museum.

[4] Marin, Sanda *(1935) Carte de Bucate*, traditional Romanian cookbook.

[5] Hebb, Donald (1949) *The Organization of Behavior,* Psychology Press.

[6] Lambert, Wallace (1972) *Language, Psychology and Culture: Essays*, Stanford University Press.

[7] Levin, Harry, and Joanna P Williams (1970) *Basic Studies in Reading,* Basic Books

[8] Johnson, RW (2021) *Foreign Native,* Jonathan Ball.

[9] Malherbe, EG (1946) *The Bilingual School: A Study of Bilingualism in South Africa,* Longmans, Green & Co.

[10] Ianco-Worrall, Anita D. (1972) *Bilingualism and Cognitive Development, J. Child Development*, Vol. 43

No 4.

[11] Worrall, Denis (2018) *The Independent Factor, My Personal Journey Through Politics and Diplomacy*, Reach Publishers.

[12] Albright, Madeleine (2005) *Madam Secretary*, Harper Perennial.

[13] Ewart-Biggs, Jane (1984) *Pay, Pack and Follow*, Weidefeld and Nicholson.

[14] Kelly, June (1984) *Canberra is a Garden,* Penclaren House.

[15] Durack, Mary (1959) *Kings in Grass Castles*, Constable.

[16] Clay, Marie (1993) *Reading Recovery Program, A Guidebook for Teachers in Training*, Heinemann.

[17] McNab, Roy (1983) *The Story of South Africa House, South Africa in Britain—The Changing Pattern*, Jonathan Ball.

[18] Norman, Lady Priscilla (1982) *In the Way of Understanding*, Foxbury Press.

[19] Worrall, Anita and Lorimer, William (1986) *Highveld, The Story of a House: The Residence of the South African Ambassador to the United Kingdom*, Perskor.

[20] Shaywitz, Sally (2003) *Overcoming Dyslexia: A New and Complete Science-Based Program for Reading Problems,* Knopf Doubleday.

[21] Snowling, Margaret and Thomson, Michael (1991) *Dyslexia: Integrating Theory and Practice*, Whurr Publishers.)

[22] Feuerstein, Reuven (1980) *Instrumental Enrichment,* University Park Press.

[23] Hayward, Carl (1982) *Bright Start, Cognitive Curriculum for Young Children*, Watertown Charlesbridge.

[24] Greenberg, Katherine (1996) *CEA Building Blocks of Thinking and Tools of Learning Cognet* University of Tennessee.

[25] Hyerle, David (2005) *Thinking Maps and Visual Tools for Transforming Information into Knowledge*, Sage Publications.

[26] Costa, Arthur L. and Kallick, Bena, eds (1986) *Learning and Leading with Habits of Mind: 16 Essential Characteristics for success*. Goodreads